Cambridge Elements

Elements in Translation and Interpreting
edited by
Kirsten Malmkjær
University of Leicester

A ZOMBIE THEORY OF TRANSLATION

Or, What is a "Revenant" Translation?

Douglas Robinson
Chinese University of Hong Kong, Shenzhen

Shaftesbury Road, Cambridge CB2 8EA, United Kingdom

One Liberty Plaza, 20th Floor, New York, NY 10006, USA

477 Williamstown Road, Port Melbourne, VIC 3207, Australia

314–321, 3rd Floor, Plot 3, Splendor Forum, Jasola District Centre, New Delhi – 110025, India

103 Penang Road, #05–06/07, Visioncrest Commercial, Singapore 238467

Cambridge University Press is part of Cambridge University Press & Assessment, a department of the University of Cambridge.

We share the University's mission to contribute to society through the pursuit of education, learning and research at the highest international levels of excellence.

www.cambridge.org
Information on this title: www.cambridge.org/9781009678186

DOI: 10.1017/9781009678223

© Douglas Robinson 2025

This publication is in copyright. Subject to statutory exception and to the provisions of relevant collective licensing agreements, no reproduction of any part may take place without the written permission of Cambridge University Press & Assessment.

When citing this work, please include a reference to the DOI 10.1017/9781009678223

First published 2025

A catalogue record for this publication is available from the British Library

ISBN 978-1-009-67818-6 Hardback
ISBN 978-1-009-67823-0 Paperback
ISSN 2633-6480 (online)
ISSN 2633-6472 (print)

Cambridge University Press & Assessment has no responsibility for the persistence or accuracy of URLs for external or third-party internet websites referred to in this publication and does not guarantee that any content on such websites is, or will remain, accurate or appropriate.

For EU product safety concerns, contact us at Calle de José Abascal, 56, 1°, 28003 Madrid, Spain, or email eugpsr@cambridge.org

A Zombie Theory of Translation

Or, What is a "Revenant" Translation?

Elements in Translation and Interpreting

DOI: 10.1017/9781009678223
First published online: November 2025

Douglas Robinson
Chinese University of Hong Kong, Shenzhen
Author for correspondence: Douglas Robinson, drobinson@cuhk.edu.cn

Abstract: In "Des Tours de Babel" Jacques Derrida brilliantly deconstructs Benjamin's 1923 essay, but in "What is a 'Relevant' Translation?" his wording suggestively hints at the possibility that Benjamin sees the source text dying and returning to life as the translation, in which only the body (not the mind, not the spirit, not the sense) of the source text survives. Smash these two brilliant theorists' ideas together and arguably what emerges is a zombie theory of translation: zombies, after all, are mindless embodied revenants. If we shift Derrida's titular question slightly, and ask "What is a 'Revenant' Translation?", one radical answer would be that it is a zombie translation. To that end this Element not only theorizes the six million Holocaust Shylock-zombies but explores that theme narratively, in a 5,000-word short story interwoven with the 20,000-word article.

Keywords: zombie, revenant, experimental translation, transference, countertransference

© Douglas Robinson 2025

ISBNs: 9781009678186 (HB), 9781009678230 (PB), 9781009678223 (OC)
ISSNs: 2633-6480 (online), 2633-6472 (print)

Contents

1	From "Relevant" to "Revenant"	1
2	What is a "Revenant" Economy?	11
3	Reanimating Shylock as a Holocaust Zombie	26
4	A Short History of Holocaust Zombies	35
5	Toward a Zombie Ecology of (Un)translatability	40
	Conclusion	64
	References	66

1 From "Relevant" to "Revenant"

As you probably know, "zombie theory" is a thing – but it's not the thing I mean here.

Standardly in usage a zombie theory is an older theory that has been discredited (has "died") but continues to hold sway (to be "undead") in people's thinking, out of collective cognitive inertia. A zombie theory is a kind of theoretical habit that needs to be kicked but keeps inexplicably climbing out of the grave and eating careless thinkers' brains.

A zombie theory of translation in that established sense might be the expectation that translation studies must confirm or disconfirm the equivalence of a translation to a source text. Gideon Toury (2012: 24–28) would insist that any text that we *assume* is a translation is *assumed* to be equivalent to some other text in some other language. Theo Hermans (2014: 6) would insist that in certain institutional contexts equivalence is "proclaimed rather than found."

To translation scholars who still hold to that zombie theory, of course, it's not a zombie theory at all, but simply the way things are.

Another example might be Donald Philippi's (1989: 680) insistence that "Whatever happens after a translator sits down at the computer, it isn't anything material. ... The translator's consciousness is not focused on any object, but is rather liberated from the world of material objects. ... Abstracted from reality, the translator operates outside the spatio-temporal system in the world of pure consciousness." Karin Littau, at any rate, presents that as basically a zombie theory (without using the term) in her white paper "Translation and the Materialities of Communication" (Littau 2016). For her "the translator is part of a material, medial and technologized ecology that shapes every aspect of mind" (85); she insists this is not just some bee in her personal bonnet: "The dominance of the 'anti-physical' paradigm," she says, "has increasingly come under scrutiny in both the humanities and the social sciences" (85).

Interestingly, there, Philippi's metaphor is ghostly ("liberated from the world of material objects"), and Littau's materialism arguably hints at another kind of revenant – an embodied and possibly zombified one (but with a mind).

What I mean by a zombie theory of translation is not this lingering on of a bad theory when it should really be dead. What I mean is a *theory of translations-as-zombies*. The two theorists who seem to be pushing us in that direction, Walter Benjamin and Jacques Derrida, do not call their approach to translation a zombie theory. My brief is that their translation-theoretical essays make more sense if we agree to call a zombie a zombie.

Six Million Shylocks: A Zombie Memoir, Part 1
By Jacques Derrida
Pseudotranslated by Douglas Robinson

I was a visitor in Venice the night it happened. Let me explain.

It was 1998. I'd been invited to address the faculty at Università di Ghetto Nuovo Venezia, the small Jewish institute of higher education founded by learned rabbis in the 1520s or 1530s, after the 1516 confinement by the Venetian Senate of all Venetian Jews in the "new ghetto" near the church of San Girolamo.

My lecture was held in the sanctuary of the Sinagoghe e Museo Ebraico di Venezia – the Hebrew Synagogue and Museum of Venice. It was a smallish but lovely room, with beautiful old frescos on the walls, much carved wood around the balconies above us (originally for the women), an ornately tiled floor, and red curtains on the windows.

Since the colloquial term for the Campo di Ghetto Nuovo (camp or campus of the new ghetto) was "the university of the Jews," it was a natural thing for the rabbis in the ghetto – "on campus" – to give lessons in the synagogue (called a Shul, or school), and to start thinking of themselves, perhaps jocularly at first, as a university. The founders belonged to the Levantine Shul, which was the wealthiest Jewish community in the Ghetto, and the one given the most freedom by the Senate, due to the significant contribution it made to the Venetian economy; but over the first century of its existence it had gradually opened its doors to the Ashkenazi (German and Italian) Jews and the "western" Sephardics as well, the Ponentines (Spaniards and Portuguese).

1.1 What is (Wrong With) "What is a 'Relevant' Translation?"?

This essay and the companion story interwoven in with it, the beginning of which you've just read, come out of a certain disgruntlement with Jacques Derrida's 1998 lecture "Qu'est-ce qu'une traduction 'relevante'?" (Derrida 1999), which I will mostly be engaging in its English translation by Lawrence Venuti as "What is a 'Relevant' Translation?" (Venuti 2001b). Kathryn

Batchelor (2023) seems to reflect a similar kind of disgruntlement in noting that Venuti's translation, published in *Critical Inquiry* and later included in the second and third editions of *The Translation Studies Reader* (Venuti 2004, 2012), has canonized the essay "as a key text in Anglophone translation studies; many a Masters student in the UK, if not further afield, finds themselves required to read it, sometimes to their own bemusement" (Batchelor 2023: 1).

Why are they bemused? Because, she suggests, "Derrida's lecture is a strange, centaur-like beast" (1).

For one thing, she says, it's not really about translation.[1] It's mainly about the themes of mercy and forgiveness as developed by Shakespeare in *The Merchant of Venice* – the topic of a two-year seminar Derrida was in the middle of giving when he delivered this lecture at the Assises de la Traduction Littéraire à Arles conference, in France. Indeed she notes that the entire discussion of *The Merchant of Venice* and mercy and justice in the 1998 talk – fully two thirds of the talk: pp. 30–45 in French (Derrida 1999), 183–97 in English translation (Venuti 2001b) – was recycled almost verbatim from the written text that Derrida was then reading to his students in the two-year seminar series, recently published in two volumes (Derrida 2019, 2020 in French, and Wills 2022, 2023 in English translation). The opening and closing frame on translation is tacked on, through the rather flimsy pretext of commenting on the possibility of translating "seasons" in the line Shakespeare gives Portia, "mercy seasons justice," with the same verb he used back in 1967 to translate Hegel's *hebt auf* "sublates": *relève*.[2] The rare minor edits he introduced into the text of the seminar were brief phrases linking the discussion of forgiveness and mercy to translation.

And for another thing, she says, the ostensible translation studies frame is "not particularly interesting, for the reflections that Derrida presents are on what Matthew Reynolds (2019: 36) terms 'Translation Rigidly Conceived,' or in

---

[1] See Batchelor (2023: 2–4) for a detailed engagement with several leading translation scholars' readings of Derrida's essay as essentially and interestingly about translation. Venuti (2001a: 170), for example, believes that the essay "can be considered Derrida's most direct intervention to date into that fledgling discipline that in Europe and elsewhere is known as 'translation studies,'" and Venuti (2003/2013: 59) insists that Derrida's piece "addresses one of the most practical themes in the history of translation theory, notably the antithesis between 'word-for-word' and 'sense-for-sense' translation which occupied such writers as Cicero and Jerome." For Venuti the long section on *The Merchant of Venice* stands as "an incisive interpretation of the role of translation" (59) in Shakespeare's play. Kathleen Davis (2001: 98–99), Hans Vermeer (2005: 116), and Emmanuelle Ertel (2011) take similar stances: that the essay is primarily about translation and has some trenchant things to say about it. [Au]

[2] The French verb *relever* can mean to lift (a skirt), to pull up (socks), to stand up or help someone stand up, to lift or right (something that has toppled over), to ride up (of clothes), to put up (hair), to raise/heighten/increase (nonphysical things), to restore or rebuild, to take up (a challenge), to react or respond to, to write up (something) or take down (a note) – but also to season (food). Metaphorically it can be used to mean to fall under (a rubric or category), to derive from, or to associate with. Effectively it is a verb and a noun of interepistemic translation (for which see Robinson 2024). [Au]

other words on 'translation (*traduction, Übersetzung, traduccion, translación*, and so forth), in the rigorous sense conferred on it over several centuries by a long and complex history in a given cultural situation' [Venuti 2001b: 179]" (quoted in Batchelor 2023: 4). Yawn.

So what is a translation scholar to do with this accidentally canonized essay, if it is this tediously pedestrian on the topic of translation?

The solution offered by one unnamed lecturer online (https://archive.nptel.ac.in/content/storage2/courses/109104050/lecture12/12_7.htm) is to celebrate the uncharacteristically pedestrian Derrida as *comfortably and reassuringly* conservative. For example, Derrida writes "A relevant translation is a translation whose economy, in these two senses, is the best possible, the most appropriating and the most appropriate possible" (Venuti 2001b: 179), and the lecturer comments:

> So by economy of translation he means a word that can capture the meaning of the original in all its widest connotations; the translation that can appropriate the meaning of the source text in as few words is a relevant translation. He further states: "every translation should be relevant by vocation. It would thus guarantee the survival of the body of the original (survival in the double sense that Benjamin gives it in 'The Task of the Translator' *[das F]ortleben* and *[das Ü]berleben*: prolonged life, continuous life, living on, but also life after death)" (199).

And it does seem, at least on a superficial reading, as if Derrida's essay from beginning to end is a championing of "relevant translation": "A relevant translation would therefore be, quite simply, a 'good' translation" (177). It's "the best possible" (179). "What the translation with the word 'relevant' also demonstrates, in an exemplary fashion, is that every translation should be relevant by vocation" (199).

It's not just "good," "the best possible"; it's "exemplary" proof that "every translation" should be *called* to be relevant.

But another way of dealing with the essay, as brilliantly exemplified by Michael G. Levine (2022), is to argue (and "show") that Derrida doesn't really mean all this tepid praise. Actually, Levine suggests, he despises relevant translation. In calling it "good" translation, "the best possible," he's paraphrasing standard views, not stating his own. He's pretending to praise a commonly accepted conservative perspective on translation, one that he himself doesn't condone and would never practice.

Why would he pretend such a thing?

Perhaps just to be fair? But then he never explicitly distances his apparent support for "relevant" translation in that way.

Perhaps to satirize that perspective? But if that's what he's doing, the satire is nowhere overtly tonalized in the written text of the talk. Maybe in Arles in 1998 he read those passages in a sarcastic tone, or accompanied them with ironic eyerolls at his audience? Certainly, we can project derisive body language onto his imagined delivery as we read those words.

Perhaps because he assumes that smart people will immediately recognize tepid praise for commonplace/marketplace assumptions about "good" translations ("the best possible") as polite irony? But Derrida's audience in Arles consisted of professional literary translators, and he repeatedly addressed them in the talk/paper as people who knew much more about professional marketplace translation than he did. Shouldn't he have assumed that they would have been trained to embrace professional translation norms uncritically, as part of the cost of making a living? Shouldn't he have worked rhetorically to *wean them away* from those assumptions, instead of simply repeating them unchallenged as truisms?

His one overt hint in this distancing direction comes a few pages in: "je ne transgresse pas un code de la bienséance ou de la modestie au titre du défi provocant," he writes, "mais de l'épreuve" (Derrida 1999: 25). As Venuti (2001b) translates that: "I don't transgress a code of decency or modesty through a provocative challenge, but through a trial" (178).[3] We'll return to the "trial" in Section 2.1; for now, note simply that he is admitting that *he is transgressing*. He doesn't say explicitly what "code" he is transgressing; he doesn't list or even mention the norms of the professional translation marketplace or "relevant translation." The noun phrase *un code de la bienséance, ou de la modestie* "the code of decency or modesty" is a deliberate and surprisingly tendentious euphemism – perhaps a *reductio ad absurdum*. It might even be read – maugre Derrida's famous politeness – as a deeply submerged *défi*

---

[3] The sentence structure in the first nine words of Venuti's English translation is Derrida's. I would have translated it "I transgress a code of decency or of modesty not as ... but as ...," indicating that he does actually transgress, just not in the way one might have thought. But Derrida does say "je ne transgresse pas un code de la bienséance": "I don't transgress a code of the well-suitedness (propriety, seemliness, etc.)." The interesting question, then, is whether sticking to Derrida's French sentence structure counts as foreignization, even though the resulting English sentence is totally idiomatic, "natural," "fluent" – even "relevant." I would venture to say, in fact, that "I don't transgress a code of decency or modesty as a provocative challenge, but as a trial" is how most native speakers of English who don't pay much attention to the logic of a sentence would say or write it. "I transgress a code of decency or modesty not as ... but as ..." would sound, perhaps, not so much foreign as overprecise, persnickety, pompous, pedantic – and many native speakers of English would no doubt consider that kind of verbal pedantry alien to their native intuitions.

I also wonder about the next four words in Venuti's translation: "through a provocative challenge" for "au titre du défi provocant." What happened to the title? It would of course have felt awkward, unidiomatic, foreign in English to render that literally as "with the title of the defiance provoking" – an effect that Venuti the foreignizer might have been expected to prefer. To be sure, though, that wouldn't be the only way to foreignize Derrida's French; indeed translating "au" in "au titre du" as "through a" is arguably foreignizing. "As a challenge" seems much more idiomatic than "through a challenge." [Au] *provocant* "provocative/defiant challenge": you professional literary translators are like a Decency League, concerned with banning obscene language and bare skin in entertainment and demanding buttoned-up modesty in social dress and comportment, or, in a professional translation context, banning "irrelevant" deviations from the strait and narrow into weird postmodern experimentations that might (im)plausibly be read as zombie translations.

Read that way, Derrida's repeated praise for "relevant translation" might well be taken as letting some air out of his audience's tires.

Michael Levine's (2022) reading of the essay is infinitely more attractive than the anonymous lecturer's, but I put scare quotes around "show" a few paragraphs ago – Levine "showing" that Derrida doesn't really mean all this tepid praise – for a reason. Levine reads every sentence of the essay far more attentively than any other commentator I've seen, with the possible exception of Hélène Cixous (Milesi 2012); but the highly persuasive evidence that he marshals for his conclusions is mostly circumstantial, based on analogues from other work by Derrida himself and others. Textual evidence for those readings taken directly from "What is a 'Relevant' Translation?" is hard to find and always requires some impressive intuitive leaps.

This passage, for example, serves as a kind of hermeneutical tipping point:

> Si la question "Qu'est-ce qu'une traduction relevante ?" ne signifie rien d'autre que la question "Qu'est-ce qu'une traduction ?" ou "Que devrait être la meilleure traduction possible ?", alors on devrait faire l'économie du mot "relevante" et l'oublier, le laisser tomber sans retard.
> Et pourtant je l'ai gardé. Pourquoi ? (Derrida 1999: 29–30)

> If the question, What is a relevant translation? signifies nothing other than the question, What is a translation? or What should the best possible translation be? then one should jettison the word "relevant" and forget it, dropping it without delay.
> And yet I have kept it. Why? (Venuti 2001b: 182)

The problem there is that *ne signifie rien d'autre* "signifies nothing other" neglects to mention the several different kinds of *autres* "others" that "What is a relevant translation?" *could* be made to signify:

(1) "*relevante*" directs our attention to a specific kind of translation that usefully differentiates it from other professionally accepted kinds;
(2) "*relevante*" signifies a defect or deficiency in the accounts Derrida gives of "relevant translation";
(3) "*relevante*" signifies a defect or deficiency in professional translation as here defined by Derrida as "relevant translation";

(4) *"relevante"* is a Latinate derivative that is problematically pulled in different and crisscrossing ways in English and French; and
(5) *"relevante"* as (4) pulled in those ways makes Derrida's title untranslatable.

Heading off that list is (1) the boring strawman "other" that Derrida seems to be implicitly rejecting in favor of (4–5), which are the only two "others" that Derrida explicitly mentions as his reasons not to *faire l'économie* "make the economy" (economize) on the word "relevant" – not *l'oublier, le laisser tomber sans retard* "to obliviate it, to let it tumble without retardment" (not to forget it, drop it). Both (4) and (5) make relevant/*relever* interesting without indicating anything about (2–3) defects or deficiency in the whole business of "relevant translation." His happiness at the (5) untranslatability of his title may be a subtle hint that Levine might be right about his take on "relevant translation," that it (5>2>3) "shies away from *l'épreuve de l'expérience*, from the dangerous ordeal" (Levine 13) of untranslatability – but Derrida doesn't draw that line. He only (arguably) hints at it.

I will also be arguing more generally that Derrida could (and perhaps should) have pushed harder on the imageries that he mobilized in the essay.

Well, that's a euphemistic way of putting it. Let's just say that my zombie reading of the essay, and the zombie memoir interwoven with it, like a pound of narrative flesh in rebarbative reverse, is an extremist strategy for exploring the possibilities that might have emerged had Derrida pushed harder.

Six Million Shylocks: A Zombie Memoir, Part 1.1
By Jacques Derrida
Pseudotranslated by Douglas Robinson

I had been invited by the Sephardic Rabbi Mois Abravanel, the rabbinic "leader" of the university.[4] We had spoken at some length on the telephone. In addition to Hebrew, Ladino, Yiddish, and Italian he spoke French and English fluently. Over the phone he struck me as an impressively learned man in Western as well as Jewish philosophy. In person he was sharp, dry as a late autumn twig, but with a subtle undercurrent of barely controlled chaos. I took to him at once.

---

[4] I can't help thinking that Abravanel is a fictional name – that Derrida didn't want to reveal the real name of the Sephardic rabbi by whose side he stood all that fateful night of the six million Shylocks. In 1979 Philip Roth published *The Ghost Writer*, with a character named Felix Abravanel, loosely based on Saul Bellow. Like Bellow, Felix Abravanel had had many marriages; his dominant humor as a character was vanity. It's clear Derrida is not basing the rabbi's character on Roth's Abravanel; but perhaps the name came to him from Roth's novel? [Tr]

Now, see? That footnote was written by the "Tr[anslator]," and appropriately marked. [Au]

But the author of that previous line in this footnote was not the purported "Au[thor]" of Derrida's zombie memoir, making that line inappropriately marked. [Tr]

As one might expect, the university had always had to struggle to stay alive. The strict controls that the Venetian Senate had imposed on the Jews had kept the community poor, and by the time Napoleon conquered the Republic of Venice and liberated the Jews (in 1797) – tore down the high walls and gates of the Ghetto (a word of Venetian origin) and made its residents full citizens – there were only 1600 inhabitants of the Ghetto. Most of them eked out a paltry living as servants, shopkeepers, and rag and bone merchants. But the Ghetto survived, as a Jewish district in Venice. It survived the Risorgimento, World War I, the years of fascism and the Sho'ah, and since World War II has arisen from the ashes, as it were – a revenant university for a revenant community. It still occupies the Ghetto, with its narrow streets and tiny squares, its five synagogues, and its small but illustrious university.

Knowing something of this history, I had decided to read my "*Qu'est-ce qu'une traduction 'revenante'*?" – a kind of hauntology of translation. What is a "revenant" translation? That paper, if you haven't read it, was mostly about my translation of Hegel's *Aufhebung* as *relève*; I discussed the *relève*, Hegel's *Aufhebung*, as a notional reliving or relifting of the Passion and Good Friday into full and total awareness. I described "the travail of mourning" that accompanies the resurrection of the revenant, the specter or the *corps glorieux* "glorious corpse" that, I say, playing on my keyword, *se lève* "rises," *se relève* "rises again," and marches (or walks: *et marche*). In passing I mentioned the line Shakespeare gives Portia in *The Merchant of Venice* that "mercy seasons justice," suggesting that *relève* could also be used to translate "seasons."

1.2 Toward "What is a 'Revenant' Translation?"

Kathryn Batchelor has an intriguing alternative to Derrida's opening pages on "Translation Rigidly Conceived," one focusing on a throwaway remark Derrida makes in his introductory paragraphs: "le mot . . . *dans le corps de sa singularité idiomatique*" (Derrida 1999: 21) "the word . . . in the body of its idiomatic singularity" (Venuti 2001b: 175, quoted in Batchelor 2023: 8). She tracks Derrida's word-oriented play with translation through a series of his other works, focusing particularly on *relève*,[5] and concludes:

---
[5] See also Bolduc (2023) for a persuasive argument in favor of focusing not on "relevant/*relève*" as "the primary relevant" but on "mercy/*merci*." For some reason, however, Bolduc doesn't mention "mercenary," which, like French *merci* and English mercy, also derives from Latin *mercēs* "reward, wages, punishment, penalty, rent, bribe." After all, if Bolduc's theme is that "Derrida presents a rhetorical ethos that embeds translation, relevance, and mercy in a personally-inflected public reflection on the 'Jewish Question' and its very real historical consequences" (449), his

Yet reading the 1998 lecture in full cognisance of this extensive network and thus with a view of *relevant* as a translative body (rather than as denoting the theoretical concept known in English as "relevance") allows us to join the apparently disjointed elements in Derrida's lecture in a different way than hitherto attempted. Rather than seeking to build on Derrida's lightly sketched analogy between the economy of translation and the economy of mercy, we can instead be attentive to how translation – through the translative body of the word relevant – "puts [languages] to work" (Venuti 2012, 384), bringing about a "writing or rewriting that is performative or poetic" (ibid.). (Batchelor 2023: 10)

My only hesitation about Batchelor's approach is that it focuses all its attention on (4–5) and doesn't engage the slippage Derrida leaves undeveloped in his argument between (2–3) and (4–5). "Rather than seeking to build on Derrida's lightly sketched analogy between the economy of translation and the economy of mercy" means that we can just ignore (2–3) the defects and deficiencies in Derrida's discussions of "relevant translation" and focus all our attention on (4–5) "how translation – through the translative body of the word relevant – 'puts [languages] to work'." That would mean ignoring not only half of the essay but half of the translationality of "the translative body of the word relevant." If the half that is ignored is the half that just drags the expected brilliance of Derrida's riffing down, no great loss. But . . .

Levine (2022) takes another tack: he complicates every aspect, every moment, in Derrida's essay by triangulating it with other writings, especially Derrida's (Bass 1987) "To Speculate – on 'Freud'" (the uncanniness of the Freudian repetition compulsion); Austin's (1962/1975) *How To Do Things With Words* (the tension between constative statements and performative actions); Freud's (1997) "Theme of the Three Caskets," to which Derrida (Venuti 2001b) alludes in passing (184n4: -phor and -fer and the -latum in translation as carrying); Jean Laplanche and Jean-Bertrand Pontalis (Nicholson-Smith 1973) in *Language of Psychoanalysis* ("the reemergence of infantile prototypes that are experienced with a strong sensation of immediacy," which "may also be

---

most explicit statement of that theme is his discussion of Portia saying "My mind was never yet more mercenary" (IV.1.436):

Nul ne saurait mieux dire le "mercenariat" du "merci" à tous les sens de ce mot. Et d'ailleurs nul ne sait jamais mieux dire que Shakespeare, lui qu'on a accusé d'antisémitisme pour une pièce qui met en scène avec une puissance inégalée tous les grands ressorts de l'antijudaïsme chrétien. (Derrida 1999: 38)

No one could better express the "mercenary" dimension of "merci" in every sense of this word. And no one could ever express it better than Shakespeare, who has been charged with anti-Semitism for a work that stages with an unequalled power all the great motives of Christian anti-Judaism. (Venuti 2001b: 191) [Au]

observed in the process of translation" [Laplanche and Pontalis 455; quoted in Levine 9]); and so on.

Along the way Levine highlights several imageries that will prove useful as we edge from "relevance" toward "revenance": the uncanny repetition of "haunting bodies and stalking ghosts" (8); "a series of ghosts standing in for others, for a structure of haunting without origin or end" (8–9); the idea that "something inside [the Hegelian dialectics] seems to work against them, something that secretly, silently, and insistently undermines and reworks them from the inside out" (13); "tongues that lick each other" (14) and the tensions between an embodied *langue*-as-tongue and a disembodied *langue*-as-language (15: "a certain licking and caressing of *la langue*"), or, as Derrida (Venuti 2001b: 199) puts it (and Levine quotes on p. 12), "what, in being freed from the body, is elevated above it, interiorizes it, spiritualizes it, preserves it in memory."

That kind of interiorized, spiritualized memory is one of the things that "revenant" zombie translation will call into question.

Six Million Shylocks: A Zombie Memoir, Part 1.2
By Jacques Derrida
Pseudotranslated by Douglas Robinson

The audience, if small, was attentive; their eyes bright, their backs straight. The Q&A, mostly in French, but with a few questions in English as well, ignited a lively discussion of uses of "lifting" that I hadn't covered in the talk, especially the connections between "lifting or pulling up" and "restoring or rebuilding," "taking up a challenge," "reacting or responding," and "writing something up." Could writing something up; could writing up the taking up of a challenge; could reacting or responding have the real-world effect of restoring or rebuilding? Did that writing-something-up work the same way in translation?

2 What is a "Revenant" Economy?

In this essay I'm going to be broaching, and in the zombie memoir I've interwoven with it boosting, an economy of *recursivity* ... a recursion specifically of revenants as disturbingly/decayingly embodied/disemminded memories ... a licking not of a lover's lips but of a bloody wound, a ravenous bite, an exposed brain ... an embodied revenant recursion that disrupts the social order of the present by repeating a repressed traumatic past, which always seems to *condition* the (narrative) past.

"To condition the (narrative) past": specifically, to (re)condition ("translate") the past-being-narrativized-as-present, history-becoming-habitualized-reality. The recursive/revenant economy that I propose to read into Derrida's essay is procedurally related to his earlier economies of supplementarity and iterability. In the recursive economy of supplementarity the supplement seems to come later and to offer the main set a belated and inadequate kind of completion, but then is repeatedly found to be *inaugurating the possibility* of imagining and organizing and limiting the main set. In the recursive economy of iterability the repeat performance of a performative utterance similarly seems to be an empty and indeed "parasitic" imitation of a "true serious" performative that precedes it, but it is repeatedly found to be conditioning the communicability of any and all performativity.

In the kind of recursive/revenant economy I track, "the quality of mercy is [repeatedly, insistently] strained."[6]

Here in Section 2 I'll expand on (Section 2.1) Derrida's "economy of inbetweenness" and "'economy' of adaptation" and (Section 2.2) the transferential economy that Michael Levine teases out of the essay, en route to (Section 2c) recursive/revenant economies. Sections 3–5 will then move us toward a specifically zombie revenant economy of translatability and untranslatability: "Reanimating Shylock as a Holocaust Zombie" in Section 3, "A Short History

---

[6] The track that batters my memory here is Michelle Shocked's "Quality of Mercy" from the soundtrack to *Dead Man Walking*. That whole soundtrack, really. The movie's title suggests the undead zombie shuffle, but of course Sean Penn doesn't play a zombie: his character is *about-to-be-dead*. But the soundtrack's disturbing brilliance keeps echoing through my enminded body as I write this essay. [Au]

of Holocaust Zombies" in Section 4, and "Toward a Zombie Ecology of (Un-) translatability" in Section 5.

Meanwhile, in the zombie memoir of our heteronymous[7] author Jacques Derrida, it is already happening.

> Six Million Shylocks: A Zombie Memoir, Part 2
> By Jacques Derrida
> Pseudotranslated by Douglas Robinson
>
> And then it began.
> "Professor Derrida," Rabbi Abravanel said, "you spoke of the *corps glorieux*, the glorious corpse or body – presumably of Jesus Christ, God the Son for G. W. F. Hegel – that rises again and walks."
> "Yes?"
> "Here at the University of the Jews we tend to speak of bodies that rise and walk but are not so glorious, such as golems."
> "Yes," I said, "certainly."
> Mysteriously, almost ritualistically, two young men in the audience began to tramp their feet.
> Symbolic golemizing?

2.1 Derrida's Economies

Derrida says he wants to explore "a certain *economy* that relates the translatable to the untranslatable, not as the same to the other, but as same to same or other to other" (Venuti 2001b: 178; Derrida's-and-then-Venuti's emphasis). One imagines a poster with a vertical line down the middle labeled "same to same or other to other," and "what is translatable" on one side and "what is untranslatable" on the other. "Relating" would then be a matter of drawing a string across from "what is translatable" to "what is untranslatable."

Not a complex image. The complication is that he wants to call it an "*economy*."

But perhaps "relat[ing] the translatable to the untranslatable" is just what high-school English teachers are apparently still calling a "thesis sentence"? Maybe he's just putting a kind of title on the idea of an economy of relation and will next set about filling in the real economic complexities?

Maybe – but he actually seems to be heading in the opposite direction. In the next paragraph it's no longer an economy but "a *principle* of economy": "How does a *principle of economy* permit one to say two apparently contradictory things at the same time (1. 'Nothing is translatable'; 2. 'Everything is

---
[7] For a theory of translational heteronyms, see Robinson (2022). [Au]

translatable)?" (179; Derrida's-and-then-Venuti's emphasis). A principle of economy, like an ideal type of economy, or the Platonic Form of "economy," is not a loose gathering of forces functioning to regulate the distribution and valuation of resources; it's an abstract structure with no possibility of play in it.

A principle of economy actually sounds less like an economic circulation and more like a principle of parsimony, or Occam's Razor: let's define translatability and untranslatability as parsimoniously as we can, for example by treating them not as opposites but as different instantiations of the same thing.

For Derrida, as for most practicing translators, the parsimonious response to loose talk of untranslatability involves reference to "the experience that I suppose is so common to us as to be beyond any possible dispute, namely, that any given translation, whether the best or the worst, actually stands between the two, between absolute relevance, the most appropriate, adequate, univocal transparency, and the most aberrant and opaque irrelevance" (178).

In other words, if "translation" is defined in one way (as the perfect target-language reproduction of every aspect of a source text, including style and word order), "nothing is translatable"; and if "translation" is defined in another way (as a pragmatic workaround that gives the target reader a pretty good idea of what is going on in the source text, without quantitative equivalence), "everything is translatable."

Derrida (1999) calls this an "économie de l'entre-deux" (26) / "economy of in-betweenness" (Venuti 2001b: 179): real-world translation would seem to be the middle excluded by a dumb binary. Not exactly earth-shaking news: this is pretty much true of every binary. And of course he didn't invent the dumb binary or the idea that real-world translation happens between the poles: the old chestnut "as freely as you must, as closely as you can" goes way back, at least to early-modern Europe. His audience in Arles was made up of practicing literary translators, who may not have known the history behind the binary but would certainly have recognized its general contours. And he addressed them as people who knew more about translating than he did.

It's a little strange, perhaps, that in roughing in the practical situation on the ground, he describes what a practicing translator would call a learned knack, a talent for workarounds,[8] a knowing how to handle semantic difficulties, as an "economy":

> To understand what this economy of in-betweenness signifies, it is necessary to imagine two extreme hypotheses, the following two hyperboles: if to a

---

[8] In my introduction to an unpublished lipogrammatic translation of Walter Benjamin's "Aufgabe des Übersetzers" I theorize lipogrammatic translation experiments as an "irrelevant" alternative to the standard professional strategy for using more words to translate a single "untranslatable" word: "a lipogrammatic translation is not just a deliberate collection of workarounds that don't quite work; it is a collection of *self-consciously highlighted* workarounds. It's a way of saying to the target reader – of bragging, really: watch me pull off the unlikeliest and least plausible of workarounds!" [Au]

translator who is fully competent in at least two languages and two cultures, two cultural memories with the sociohistorical knowledge embodied in them, you give all the time in the world, as well as the words needed to explicate, clarify, and teach the semantic content and forms of the text to be translated, there is no reason for him to encounter the untranslatable or a remainder in his work. (Venuti 2001b: 179)

That is actually just the first hyperbole: perfect "free" translation, which conveys the whole sense and style of the original by straying at will from its quantitative word count, sentence count, paragraph count. The other is perfect "close" translation, which captures the exact meaning and style of the original with the exact same sentence structures and each word translated accurately and without remainder.

Because real-world translation falls into the middle between those impossible extremes – those "hyperboles" – it is never either perfectly free or perfectly close. This is obviously what Derrida calls "translation (*traduction, Übersetzung, traduccion, translación*, and so forth), in the rigorous sense conferred on it over several centuries by a long and complex history in a given cultural situation" (179) – and nobody needs him to tell us that. This is the domain in which Derrida tells us hardly anything about translation, and in which what he does tell us is him belaboring the obvious, knowledge that is "relevant" only to undergraduate students taking their first class on translation.

But now consider the passing hints that Michael Levine gathers from here and there in Derrida's text and reads as a more trenchant sketch of an economy that produces "relevant" translations:

> That his own translation of *Aufhebung* as *relève* has proven to be "relevant" and "a good translation" no doubt bothers Derrida – "bothers" him in the sense of provoking, irritating, and unsettling him, which is to say it fascinates him. What also seems to bother him is the implicit connection he notices between a translation deemed "relevant" and an "economy" of adaptation, success, validity, adequate compensation, debt payment, the possible, and the most possible. (Levine 2022: 13)

This is a good first step past the tired platitudes: rather than simply defining "relevant translation" as "good," "the best possible," Derrida feels uneasy about that relevant "goodness." Derrida nowhere overtly confesses that botheredness, that provocation, that irritation, that unsettlement, that fascination; that's all speculation. But it's productive speculation. It organizes the hints to which Levine directs our attention in plausible and attractive ways. In those hints Derrida is still somewhere in the middle between extreme hypotheses, but he is more forthcoming about what he wants to happen in that middle. Instead of being just vaguely *dans l'entre-deux* "in the in-between," he insists on *courting* impossibility, courting untranslatability. His rejoinder to the marketplace tolerance for "the most possible" is effectively Goethe's advice in the *Maximen und Reflexionen* (which Derrida didn't cite, or perhaps even know): the translator must "bis ans Unübersetzliche herangehen; alsdann wird man aber erst die fremde Nation und die fremde Sprache gewahr" (Goethe 1826/1907: 449), or "quest toward the untranslatable: there you will catch your first glimpse of the foreign country and its language" (Robinson 2014: 224). The impossible ideal for Goethe isn't translatability but untranslatability (in modern German *die Unübersetzbarkeit*; in Goethe's German *die Unübersetzlichkeit*). As it did for the Romantics and Walter Benjamin before him, for Derrida too that seems to mean radical literalism – tellingly, something like the perfection of "close" translation that adheres strictly to the extreme hypothesis that makes translation (seem) impossible, but now as a deranging tool rather than an ideal. Ply the waters of *l'entre-deux* "the in-between" by steering away from marketplace tolerance for lowered expectations and mobilizing the opposite extreme, word-for-word perfection, as a *complication*.

Like Goethe, Derrida knows that he will never reach that goal, but no matter: the tricky pleasure lies in the approach. That approach begins to stir hints of the impossible ideal into the mundanity of "relevant" translation, enlivening it by hybridizing it. Or in Derrida's terms, "it puts to work the languages, first of all, without adequation or transparency, here assuming the shape of a new writing or rewriting that is performative or poetic" (Venuti 2001b: 198). "Without adequation or transparency": remember that "the most appropriate, adequate, univocal transparency" was Derrida's characterization of what he called "absolute relevance" (178). (This is one of those rare moments in the essay when Derrida distances himself clearly from "relevant translation." But even that "clarity" is only available through *une épreuve* "a test": you have to have a good enough memory to recognize "without adequation or transparency" as a callback to a brief list of attributes twenty pages earlier.)[9]

Levine (2022) calls that "performative or poetic" approach *l'expérience de l'impossible* and notes that Derrida calls it *une épreuve* "an ordeal" involving

---

[9] Derrida discusses memory as a liberation from the body: "what, in being freed from the body, is elevated above it, interiorizes it, spiritualizes it, preserves it in memory" (Venuti 2001b: 199). In Section 4 we will be reading Elana Gomel's theorization of zombies as another kind of memory, a kind that is fiercely and overwhelmingly embodied, reduced to a disgustingly disenminded embodiment. The interesting question here is whether the critical analysis of Derrida's talk/paper is perfectly or completely "freed from the body" and "elevated above it," or whether it still relies heavily on embodiment. What occurs to me is that when I type a quotation like "the most appropriate, adequate, univocal transparency," and then, later, type "without adequation or transparency," doesn't the physical activity of typing enhance my memory and thus by extension my critical attentiveness? Isn't this notion that memory is a liberation from the body wishful thinking primed by bad (binary mind–body) theory? [Au]

"experimentation": "A 'relevant' translation, one satisfied by the most possible, *le plus possible*, shies away from *l'épreuve de l'expérience*, from the dangerous ordeal, the testing and experimentation that every attempt at translation conceived of as an 'experience of the impossible' should be" (13).

What specifically should that experience be? "Comme ce qui est dû à Shylock, l'insolvable même," Derrida (1999: 21) says: "Much like what is owed to Shylock, insolvency itself" (Venuti 2001b: 175).

> Parler, enseigner, écrire (ce dont je fais aussi profession et qui au fond, comme beaucoup d'entre vous ici, m'engage corps et âme presque tout le temps), je sais que cela n'a de sens à mes yeux que dans l'épreuve de la traduction, à travers une expérience que je ne distinguerai jamais d'une expérimentation. (Derrida 1999: 21)

> Speaking, teaching, writing (which I also consider my profession and which, after all, like many here among you, engages me body and soul almost constantly) – I know that these activities are meaningful in my eyes only in the proof [*l'épreuve:* trial or ordeal] of translation, through an experience that I will never distinguish from experimentation. (Venuti 2001b: 175)

Or, as we've seen him putting it:

> Il reste que, faites-m'en le crédit, je ne transgresse pas un code de la bienséance ou de la modestie au titre du défi provocant, mais de l'épreuve : pour soumettre l'expérience de la traduction à l'épreuve de l'intraduisible. (Derrida 1999: 25)

> What remains is that—trust me—I don't transgress a code of decency or modesty through a provocative challenge, but through a trial [*mais de l'épreuve*], by submitting the experience of translation to the trial of the untranslatable [*pour soumettre l'expérience de la traduction à l'épreuve de l'intraduisible*]. (Venuti 2001b: 178)

Is that self-testing, that experimental self-propulsion into danger, an economy? Probably not. But now we're getting somewhere interesting. The static structure of the purported *économie de l'entre-deux* "economy of the in-between" imposes that restrictive *code de la bienséance, ou de la modestie* "code of decency or modesty" on the market-conscious translator, who compliantly creates a "relevant" translation, which is to say a "good" translation, "the best possible." As we've seen, that "decency" or "modesty" requires that the market-conscious translator steer clear of Derridean postmodern "irrelevancy," the kind of experimentalism that takes the compliant translator's eyes off the prize (income, a livelihood, or Latin *mercēs*). But the wrench that Derrida tosses into the workings of that code is not a "provocative challenge" so much as a test, a trial, an ordeal, *une épreuve* – one that he creates for himself, to push *his* translations beyond boring "relevance."

Then again, what is "the untranslatable," exactly? Most commonly it refers to a word or a phrase or a whole source text that commentators view as impossible to translate adequately, without remainder; but that can't be what Derrida means here. He means not a specific text but an abstraction, or perhaps a felt kinesthesis, an aporia, standing in for a nebulously defined but strongly felt translation strategy. His "transgression" is more or less the opposite of the untranslatable text: his source text could be translated "relevantly," which is to say "well," "the best way possible," or piously, decently, modestly, respectably, but he would find the result of that "bestness" distasteful. He doesn't want to yield to that marketplace norm, which to him feels like a pious dumbing down, a decent or modest condescension, a case of the bland leading the bland. He wants to push himself to translate more complexly, indeed more problematically, more aporetically. He musters up a strategy that he calls *l'épreuve de l'intraduisible* "the trial of the untranslatable" to goad him into that problematized or aporetic zone where the available words and phrases are not what the marketplace would consider "relevant." He wants to *deprive* himself, "relieve" himself, of the usual idiomatic resources that feed the marketplace zone of relevant translation, in order to intensify the performative/poetic feel of the work.[10]

That aporetic trial zone is what I want to call the zombie zone.

Six Million Shylocks: A Zombie Memoir, Part 2.1
By Jacques Derrida
Pseudotranslated by Douglas Robinson

"As I'm sure you know," the old rabbi went on, "the word *golem* appears in the Scripture, in Psalm 139: 16, where God refers to גלמי *golmi* 'my golem,' or 'my light form,' or 'my raw material' to mean the half-finished human being He is creating."

"I remember reading something about that," I nodded. "And, in later texts, such as the Mishnah, a 'golem' is a stupid person, or perhaps an uncultivated person."

---

[10] As I wrote in Footnote 8, one way of thinking about the justification for lipogrammatic translation is that, faced with the common problem that there is no term in the target language that covers all the relevant semantic fields in the source-language term, traditional translators typically minimize or uneasily ignore the problem, but lipogrammatic translators intensify the problem. We use various strategic constraints to narrow the pool of words and phrases from which rough equivalents might be found. Ideally, we reduce the size of that pool for every possible target-language equivalent to zero, or as near to zero as we can manage. This strategy I call "infinitesimal (dis)opportunity. The infinite approach to impossibility."

Of course Derrida is not doing lipogrammatic translation. His preference for going through *l'épreuve de l'intraduisible* "the trial of the untranslatable" is only one strategy of experimental translation – only one entrance point into the aporetic/zombie zone. [Au]

"Right."

"Not exactly a revenant," I said.

"No. A new creation."

"The golem rises," I said, "but does not rise again. Just once."

"No *relève*," the old rabbi agreed. He throttled a cough so that it sounded like a death rattle. "And no glorious body. But there are certain similarities nonetheless. The golem rises, apparently from the dead, but actually from the dust, from inanimate matter, and walks."

2.2 Levine's Transferential Economy

Beyond that emphasis on "the experience of the impossible/untranslatable" as an "ordeal," Levine tends to read Derrida symptomatically, as driven by various unconscious formations to obsess about certain things and to ignore others:

> As a translator, Derrida is fated to act in certain ways. Haunted by the words of William Shakespeare (and later by those of G.W.F. Hegel), he is made to speak the language of avowal and fatality (*avouer* and *voué*), the language of confession and even that of Shakespeare's Portia (echoing in the verb "*porter sur*" and all the other verbs bearing on bearing). In other words, he seems to be ventriloquized by the language and economy, by a certain language of economy, he seeks to translate from *The Merchant of Venice*. Accentuating the root of "bearing" but also of "carrying," he subtly draws attention to the way the very word and act of "translation" will have borne "transference," will have been affected, inhabited, and displaced by it from the very first. This, I would suggest, is the "self-contradiction" of which he speaks. (Levine 2022: 7)

"Fated," "haunted," and "ventriloquized": three verbs that subtly nudge us toward a recursive/revenant economy in Section 2c and ultimately toward a zombie economy of translation in Sections 5c–5g. So when Derrida rambles strangely about a principle of economy or an economy of the in-between, when he seems to be lost and confused and mostly mouthing painfully obvious platitudes, that is because he has been translating "a certain language of economy … from *The Merchant of Venice*," and that language has been ventriloquizing him. He's not in control. He's the ventriloquist's dummy, and thus not to blame for any dumb remarks at which we may be gaping.

As for "subtly drawing attention" to transference, to the "bearing" of transference, Derrida first hints in this direction early in the essay:

> Je soulignerais *laborieuse* pour announcer quelques mots en *tr*.—et que le motif du *labour*, du *tr*avail d'accouchement mais aussi du *tr*avail *tr*ansférentiel et *tr*ansformationnel, dans tous les codes possibles et non seulement dans celui de la psychanalyse, entrera en concurrence avec le

> motif apparemment plus neutre de la *tr*aduction, comme *tr*ansaction et comme *tr*ansport. (Derrida 1999: 23)

> I underline *laborious* to announce several words in *tr.* and to indicate that the motif of labor, the *tr*avail of childbirth, but also the *tr*ansferential and *tr*ansformational *tr*avail, in all possible codes and not only that of psychoanalysis, will enter into competition with the apparently more neutral motif of *tr*anslation, as *tr*ansaction and as *tr*ansfer. (Venuti 2001b: 176)

The hint there that "translation," as *le* motif *apparemment plus neutre* "an apparently more neutral *motif*," will be competitively influenced by transference "in all possible codes and not only that of psychoanalysis" leads Levine (2022) to "the way the very word and act of 'translation' will have borne 'transference,' will have been affected, inhabited, and displaced by it from the very first" (7).

But note how deftly Levine sidesteps transference's psychoanalytical "code." Derrida declines to restrict transference to that code, but he also declines to exclude it. And it should go without saying that that psychoanalytical code would entail the unconscious transfer of affect not simply from one word or "motif" to another but from one person to another.

It would not, in other words, be just "the very word and act of 'translation'" that would have been "affected, inhabited, and displaced by [transference] from the very first." It would also be the affective body of Derrida himself.

Who then, we might ask next, would be the parental figure whose emotions and desires might notionally have been unconsciously transferred to Derrida? Levine seems to hint that it is Shakespeare, or *The Merchant of Venice* as Shakespeare's authoritative word. That would be the sense in which Derrida is "haunted" and "ventriloquized" by the play: "affected, inhabited, and displaced" by it.

In suggesting that Derrida is "haunted" by Hegel's ghost, too, Levine is hinting at another kind of transference: Hegel not just as an influential philosopher whom Derrida has deconstructed, but as a revenant that lurks inside Derrida's *Geist*.

> A case in point is the concept of *Aufhebung* itself. Inhabited by competing forces, it offers resistance first and foremost to itself, which is to say that even when the prevailing power structures – like those associated with Hegelian dialectics – remain intact, something inside them seems to work against them, something that secretly, silently, and insistently undermines and reworks them from the inside out. Derrida seeks to flesh out this internal resistance, this resistance inherent in the very movement of the Hegelian *Aufhebung*. (Levine 2022: 12–13)

I'm going to be linking that "something that secretly, silently, and insistently undermines and reworks them from the inside out" not just with revenants but specifically with zombies – zombies irrepressibly popping up out of secret underground passageways. That "something" keeps "secretly, silently, and insistently" returning and resisting, like traumatically repressed memories.

But that's not all. Derrida himself later writes:

> Il y a d'abord un serment (oath), un engagement intenable, avec risque de parjure, une dette et un devoir qui constituent le ressort même de l'intrigue, du *plot* et du complot. Or il serait facile de montrer (et j'avais tenté de le faire ailleurs) que toute traduction implique cet endettement insolvable et ce serment de fidélité envers un original donné – avec tous les paradoxes d'une telle loi et d'un tel engagement, de ce lien (bond) et de ce contrat, de cet engagement d'ailleurs impossible et dissymétrique, transférentiel et contre-transférentiel, comme un serment voué à la trahison et au parjure. (Derrida 1999 : 31)

> First there is an oath, an untenable promise, with the risk of perjury, a debt and an obligation that constitute the very impetus for the intrigue, for the plot, for the conspiracy [*complot*]. Now it would be easy to show (and I have tried to do so elsewhere) that all translation implies an insolvent indebtedness and an oath of fidelity to a given original – with all the paradoxes of such a law and such a promise, of a bond and a contract, of a promise that is, moreover, impossible and asymmetrical, transferential and countertransferential, like an oath doomed to treason or perjury. (Venuti 2001b: 183)

Antonio is the play's main figure of *endettement insolvable* "insolvent indebtedness," and also of the *serment de fidélité envers un original donné* "oath of fidelity to a given original," namely Shylock's bond *[lien]*: "Let me have judgment," he says, "and the Jew his will" (IV.1.81). He agreed to the bond that would take his life if he defaulted; now that he has defaulted, he is ready to die. Derrida is reading that insolvent indebtedness and that oath of fidelity as a figure of "all translation" – which is to say that Antonio is a figure for every translator. But for whom else?

Certainly for Derrida himself as a translator. But what about Derrida as the author of this essay?

That last question becomes especially pressing in the part about "a promise that is, moreover, impossible and asymmetrical, transferential and countertransferential." Transference, as we've seen, is not to be limited to a psychoanalytical "code": the Latin roots of transference have been around for more than two millennia, in the "codes" of transport, property deeds, and so on. But countertransference was expressly theorized for the first and definitive time *for* that psychoanalytical "code" – by Freud himself, in 1910, as *die Gegenübertragung* – and has only ever been extended beyond that "code" metaphorically.

If we begin with Derrida-the-translator and Derrida-the-author transferring his/their affects to other people, we may find Derrida's identification with

Shylock and disidentification from Portia invested in his attitudes toward his audience in Arles. The (notional) submerged hostility of "I transgress a code of decency or modesty not through a provocative challenge, but through a trial" (Venuti 2001b: 178), implicitly calling that audience *esclaves des bienséances* "slaves to respectability," is really more intense than it needs to be with this room full of strangers. Decency, modesty, respectability, and mercy. The transference of Antonio's "insolvent indebtedness" to "all translation" and thus all translators may not be transferential in the strict psychoanalytic sense, since Derrida (1985; Graham 1985) made a similar case in reading Benjamin's "Task" in "Des Tours de Babel" a decade and a half earlier. But if there is a promise that is not only "impossible and asymmetrical" but "transferential *and countertransferential*," and that promise is therefore somehow lodged in the relationship between Derrida-the-analysand and some other-as-analyst, who is that other?

One could imagine that authoritative other as Portia, perhaps. Levine (2022) refers to Derrida being haunted and ventriloquized by "the language of confession and even that of Shakespeare's Portia (echoing in the verb '*porter sur*' and all the other verbs bearing on bearing)" (7) – but that would clearly be transference, not countertransference. Given the fact that Portia and Derrida exist in different "codes" – Portia in the "code" or fictional "frame" of written drama and stage performance, Derrida in the "code" of "real life" – it is difficult to imagine her transferring her unconscious feelings to him. Portia can be interpreted as a living human being, and therefore also as a psychoanalyst, whose "analysand" is not only Shylock but her husband Bassanio,[11] and the duke, and all of Venice – and it would even be possible to imagine her as an analyst with Derrida on the couch. But that would all be *transference*, at work in Derrida's unconscious (or ours). In that scenario it would be considerably more difficult to imagine countertransference at work. What unconscious feelings might we picture Portia harboring for Derrida the Jew, and how might we imagine those feelings skewing her judgment as she frees Antonio from Shylock and strips Shylock of all his possessions and his human dignity in the name of Christian mercy?

A more plausible stand-in for the other-as-analyst to Derrida-as-analysand, I suggest, would be "the reader," any reader – but especially perhaps Michael Levine. He does, after all, brilliantly mobilize Freudian psychoanalysis in the service of teasing out Derrida's unconscious proclivities, and thus of

---

[11] When Bassanio tells Antonio that he loves his wife as dearly as he does his own life, but would sacrifice her, give her over to Shylock to do with as he would, to deliver his friend, Portia remarks aside: "Your wife would give you little thanks for that / If she were by to hear you make the offer" (IV.1.294–301). [Au]

complicating the platitudinous obfuscations that here and there seem to "mar" and "hinder" Derrida's usual brilliance. If we were to envision a session with Levine as the shrink and Derrida on the couch, we might also explore Levine's countertransferential inclination to give Derrida all manner of little breaks. Compared with Kathryn Batchelor's and my own more disgruntled reading of Derrida's essay, Levine seems determined to mobilize the unconscious tendencies he identifies in and behind Derrida's essay to the end of protecting Derrida against possible accusations of being boring or ill-informed about translation. In Bakhtin's (1929/1984) terms, Levine-the-psychoanalyst double-voices Derrida in order to "stylize" him, to enhance the force and intelligence of his talk. What lurks (countertransferentially) just behind the boring parts and the apparently ill-informed parts is the usual Derridean brilliance.

Six Million Shylocks: A Zombie Memoir, Part 2.2
By Jacques Derrida
Pseudotranslated by Douglas Robinson

"Are you suggesting there are parallels between the golem and the Christians' resurrected deity?" I asked.

"I'm wondering," the rabbi said slowly, "whether the kind of revenant translation you sketched in your paper is more like the glorious talking embodied revenant Jesus Christ or more like the dusty clayey speechless embodied golem of the Jews."

"A very good question," I said. "An important question." I thought for a moment. "I suppose I would say that it's more like a golem, in the sense that a revenant translation for me is a body whose 'mind' or 'spirit' has been disrupted in some critical way."

"Disrupted?"

"If the 'mind' or 'spirit' of the source text is its 'sense,' its 'meaning,' its desire to communicate something to the reader, the source text dies and returns from the dead as the revenant translation."

"I see."

A young woman stood and walked stealthily to the window. Her eyes scanned the square. What was she seeing?

2.3 Recursive/Revenant Economies

But there is another way of reading that (counter)transferential economy that Levine identifies in the interstices of Derrida's essay, the way "the word and act of translation" is "affected, inhabited, and displaced" by transference – or, reading that euphemistic paraphrase "the word and act of translation" (i.e., excluding

Derrida himself from the transference) as Levine's countertransference to Derrida, the way *Derrida's mobilization* of translation is *repeatedly* or *recurringly* "affected, inhabited, and displaced" by transference.

In Section 2.2 I suggested that Portia might be interpreted as the analyst who countertransfers unconscious affects to Derrida as her analysand, but noted that the two of them occupy different "codes" or "frames." That reminded me of the moment in Derrida's famous deconstruction of John Searle in "Limited Inc a b c" (Weber and Mehlman: 1977/1988) when he quotes Searle protesting that "we do not, for example, hold the actor responsible today for the promise he made on stage last night in the way we normally hold people responsible for their promises" (88–89), and corrects him: "It would not be the actor who should be held responsible but rather the speaker committed by the promise *in the scene*, that is, the character. And indeed, he is held responsible in the play and in the *ideal* – i.e. in a certain way *fictional* – analysis of a promise" (89).

Yes, obviously. But it is equally obvious that that shining stable "real"-versus-"fictional" binary is not particularly Derridean. I read it as Derrida implying something like *"in the rationalist Enlightenment philosophy to which Searle obviously gravitates*, it would not be the actor who should be held responsible but rather the speaker committed by the promise in the scene, that is, the character." He would, in other words, be condescendingly doing Searle a favor – helping Searle keep his rationalist categories and hierarchies straight – doing Searle's conservative philosophical work for him, since poor benighted Searle seems to be incapable of doing it for himself.

Where Derrida himself, in his own name, goes with that same apparent binary is that the reperformance of a "serious" performative on stage only *seems* to be secondary, belated, supplemental. In actuality all manner of reperformance, not just on stage but "in real life," creates the conditions of possibility that make it possible for "serious" performatives to communicate:

> A standard act depends as much upon the possibility of being repeated, and thus potentially [*eventuellement*] of being mimed, feigned, cited, played, simulated, parasited, etc., as the latter possibility depends upon the possibility said to be opposed to it. And both of them "depend" upon the structure of iterability which, once again, undermines the simplicity of the oppositions and alternative distinctions. It blurs the simplicity of the line dividing inside from outside, undermines the order of succession or of dependence among the terms, prohibits (prevents and renders illegitimate) the procedure of exclusion. Such is the law of iterability. (Derrida 1977/1988: 91–92)

In other words, while Searle commonsensically follows Austin in believing that the "serious" performative comes first and any reperformance comes second and is parasitical on the "serious" performative that it imitates/follows,

Derrida is not simply proposing to make the reperformance come first. It's not the *existence* of a *single* actual reperformance that *comes first*; it's the *possibility* of reperformance *in general* that *conditions* every "serious" performative. If an utterance must be iterable in order to communicate, if every promise must be repeatable in order to count as a promise, the transition(ality) from performance to reperformance and from reperformance to performance must be built into the very communicability of any utterance.

Apply that law, now, to transference, or to the transferential economy that Michael Levine so brilliantly teases out of Derrida's essay. It's not that the translator translating or the writer writing comes first, in the fullness of Enlightenment rationality, and then is belatedly "corrupted" by transference and/or countertransference. It's not that the goal of (psycho)analysis should be to "purify" transference and countertransference *out of* the therapeutic session or other discursive encounter, and so to "restore" some imagined rationalist (super)ego-forthrightness that has been "corrupted" by the unconscious. Rather, it's that all analysis, all therapy, indeed all understanding in non-therapeutic as well as therapeutic settings emerges, is constantly emerging out of unconscious (counter)transference, and that the goal of therapy and other embodied and situated talking and knowing is to become aware of that inevitability – of that *uncanny, iterably emergent repetition*.

As I've been hinting, I want to call that kind of economy a *recursive* economy – an economy of recurrence – in which what recurs is a Latin *recurs* ("recourse"): a coursing back/again; a renewed course; a return or a recurrence. What recurs in a recurrence is recurrence, return, recourse.

It might also be called a *revenant* economy: an economy of returns, either from away or from the dead. A revenant in secular terms is a returner, a prodigal; in mythological terms it is a thing reborn, a phoenix. In horror contexts it is a zombie or a ghost that returns from the dead. ("Who you gonna call?")

A zombie economy would be a special case of a revenant economy: compare Michael Levine calling Derrida "haunted" by Hegel, which is already one step beyond what Derrida himself says, in the passage I quoted earlier: "the *relève*, Hegel's *Aufhebung*, [being] explicitly a speculative *relève* of the Passion and Good Friday into absolute knowledge, the travail of mourning also describes, preserved in its grave, the resurrection of the ghost or of the glorious body that rises, rises again [*se relève*] – and walks." "One important way to gauge the radicality of Derrida's transferential praxis," Levine (2022) adds, "is to examine the place it makes for haunting bodies and stalking ghosts. These are not only the specters of what once was but a series of ghosts standing in for others, for a structure of haunting without origin or end" (8–9).

That would be a revenant economy without zombies – and that is more or less where Derrida ends his essay, very briefly; very much in "passing" (from Hegel to the endnotes). Where he begins the essay is quite different: there his concern is with the links between *relève* and the English word "relevant," which is not yet quite French (but apparently is being introduced into French, as a loan word). Imagine a triangle, with *relève* at the top, "relevant" at the bottom left, and *Aufhebung* at the bottom right. In a sense the structure of Derrida's essay is from left to right, from "relevant" to *Aufhebung*, like a pendulum swing from the pivot point of *relève*.

In terms Derrida never uses, it would be a movement from a relevant economy to a revenant economy.

But now let's narrow revenant economies to those horrifically embodied revenants called zombies.

Six Million Shylocks: A Zombie Memoir, Part 2.3
By Jacques Derrida
Pseudotranslated by Douglas Robinson

"And rather than simply transferring the 'sense' from the dying text to the revenant," I said, "I believe in subjecting that 'sense' to the trial of the untranslatable."

Rabbi Abravanel stood unmoving for a good half minute, then furrowed his brow and templed his fingers.

"Which is what, exactly?" he asked.

"A semantic wrench that I seek to throw into the works," I said, miming the turning of a wrench. "I want to complicate the translation process, cut myself off from the most obvious and therefore most nugatory semantic resources, derail the translation project into an aporetic zone where very little is possible."

"An aporia? An impasse?"

He pushed his right fist into his left palm. Three or four of his flock mimicked the movement, watching him intently.

"Yes. A kind of imaginary or projected roadblock that requires a detour into the realm of the experimental."

"And you think of that as creating a golem translation?"

"I suppose. I had never put it in those terms before. But the idea of the golem as being unable to speak appeals to me, as a metaphor for translation. The revenant is mentally or spiritually impaired. No voice, no sense."

3 Reanimating Shylock as a Holocaust Zombie

3.1 Life After Death

In the block extract quotation from the anonymous lecturer in Section 1.1 there was an interesting moment that I forbore to comment on there, saving it instead for here: the place where Derrida brings Walter Benjamin into the conversation. "It would thus guarantee the *survival* of the body of the original," Derrida writes, and then adds parenthetically: "(*survival* in the double sense that Benjamin gives it in 'The Task of the Translator,' *[das F]ortleben* and *[das Ü]berleben*: prolonged life, continuous life, living on, but also life after death)" (Venuti 2001b: 199; Derrida's-and-then-Venuti's emphasis).

What makes that interesting is that Benjamin scholars have long rejected translations of *das Überleben* as "the afterlife" in English, here *vie par-delà la mort* in French, or, as Venuti translates Derrida, "life after death." According to the scholars, Benjamin *does not* mean that the source text dies and is reborn in and as the translation (see Robinson 2023: 36–37). But what if Derrida is hinting at something more? Even if the scholars are right about Benjamin's intended meaning, in other words, what if this apparently misleading translation of *das Überleben* is directly *relevant* to Derrida's half-hidden theme in the article ("buried" in the final sentence of the main text, to be "exhumed" here in this book) of death and revivification?

> J'insiste sur la dimension chrétienne. Outre toutes les traces que le christianisme a laissées dans l'histoire de la traduction et du concept normative de traduction, outre le fait que la relève, l'Aufhebung d'un Hegel (dont il faut toujours rappeler qu'il fut un penseur très luthérien, sans doute comme Heidegger), est explicitement une relève de la Passion et du Vendredi saint spéculatif dans le savoir absolu, le travail du deuil décrit aussi, à travers la Passion, à travers la mémoire hantée par le corps perdu mais gardé dans le dedans de son tombeau, la résurrection du spectre ou du corps glorieux qui se lève, se relève – et marche. (Derrida 1999: 47)
>
> I insist on the Christian dimension. Apart from all the traces that Christianity has left on the history of translation and the normative concept of translation, apart from the fact that the *relève*, Hegel's *Aufhebung* (one must never forget that he was a very Lutheran thinker, undoubtedly like Heidegger), is

explicitly a speculative *relève* of the Passion and Good Friday into absolute knowledge, the travail of mourning also describes, preserved in its grave, the resurrection of the ghost or of the glorious body that rises, rises again [*se relève*] – and walks. (Venuti 2001b: 199–200)

A ghost would be a revenant but would not mark "the survival of the *body*" (199; emphasis switched). The "glorious body that rises" would presumably be Jesus, a mythological revenant whose body does survive, like the phoenix, but with nail holes in his hands and feet and Easter Sunday in mind. (Though I don't remember the Bible saying that his revenant body gave off heavenly light: *glorieux* "glorious.")[12]

What interests me here is the revivification of a disgusting undead body that rises, rises again – and shambles.

Six Million Shylocks: A Zombie Memoir, Part 3.1
By Jacques Derrida
Pseudotranslated by Douglas Robinson

"This is of course very Kabbalistic," Rabbi Abravanel said.

"Y-y-yes . . ." I thought for another moment. Then, the answer coming to me suddenly: "In Walter Benjamin's version of the Kabbalah, of course," I said. "Yes. The source text is alive because it harbors the divine spark of the Tzimtzum, the constriction and condensation of the Ein Sof, but the human translator is incapable of transferring that spark to the translation, so the translation is dead – or undead."

"Undead?" my genial interlocutor smiled. "You mean it's a zombie?"

3.2 Whose?

But whose undead body?

Shylock's.

Shylock in the play? He doesn't die in the play!

Imagine Shylock dying after the end of the play and being reanimated as a zombie centuries later. Maybe tomorrow. Shylock "returning" in the sequel as a Holocaust zombie. As six million Holocaust zombies.

---

[12] It wouldn't be Lazarus either, who lies stinking in the grave for four days before Jesus resurrects him; but Jesus does refer to his raising of Lazarus from the dead as "seeing the glory of God":

> Jesus said, Take ye away the stone. Martha, the sister of him that was dead, saith unto him, Lord, by this time he stinketh: for he hath been dead four days.

> Jesus saith unto her, Said I not unto thee, that, if thou wouldest believe, thou shouldest see the glory of God? (John 11.39–40, KJV)

Thanks to Kathryn Batchelor for directing my attention to this passage. [Au]

But Shylock wasn't killed in a Nazi gas chamber. How can he be a Holocaust zombie?[13]

Six Million Shylocks: A Zombie Memoir, Part 3.2
By Jacques Derrida
Pseudotranslated by Douglas Robinson

As the good rabbi voiced that last word, "zombie," there came a crash and a clatter from inside one wall.

All heads turned to the venerable rabbi with whom I had been chatting.

"Rabbi Abravanel," one of the other elders said carefully, "have you made another golem?"

Rabbi Abravanel paused briefly before answering: "No. Certainly not."

"Then?"

Rabbi Abravanel looked grave. "I don't know," he said.

More noises came from inside the wall. It sounded like someone tripping over a mountain of meat cleavers in the dark.

Then, the snapping of wood, and the screaming of ancient rusty nails as they were yanked out of a wall.

Huffing and snorting.

There was, it seemed to me, there must be, a largish living thing just behind the wall.

"Is there, perhaps," I ventured, "a doorway there? Could a bardot, or, I don't know, a bison be trapped in a storage room?"[14]

---

[13] Notice the pivot here: in almost the exact center of the book we shift from theory to practice, real ideality to ideal reality, imaginary imagined zombies to real imagined zombies. And what brings about the metaontological shift? The rabbi's *speaking of the word* "zombie." That's metacritifiction at its finest. [Au]

[14] I don't know what to make of this exchange. Bison and bardots in Venice? Both exist in Europe, though only about a thousand bison survive today, and bardots are extremely rare. And don't think I mistranslated: Derrida has *bison* in French; the European bison is *bisonte* in Spanish and Italian. Unless these are false friends, and it was actually a large bird? [Tr]

But then what is a bardot? Apart from Mlle. Bridget (b. 1934)? [Ed]

Sorry, a *bardot* in French is a hinny in English. I thought it sounded better in French. Hinny, ninny, you know. [Tr]

And what is a hinny? [Ed]

The offspring of a male horse and a female donkey. [Tr]

So a mule? [Ed]

No, a mule is the offspring of a male donkey and a female horse. [Tr]

Why have I never heard of a hinny? [Ed]

As I say, they're very rare. They're difficult to breed. Horses have 64 chromosomes, donkeys only 62. Also, male horses just don't find female donkeys attractive. You see the problem. [Tr]

Side question: what is a zorse? [Ed]

Offspring of a zebra and a horse. As opposed to the offspring of a zebra and a donkey, called a zedonk. [Tr]

"We don't get many bison in Venice these days," an older woman in the second row sighed, seeming not to notice the uneasiness my question had provoked in the small sanctuary. "I had a pet baby bison as a young girl. It got too big. We had to get rid of it."

"Did you get rid of it in this synagogue?" a young man asked her, quite seriously.

"Why," the woman replied, her eyes going wide, "no! Of course not. We ..." She paused. "We took it to Spain."

"To Spain?"

"To the European bison reserve in San Cebrián de Mudá, in the Montaña Palentina."[15]

3.3 Reading Shylock's Experiences as Anticipations of the Holocaust

Think of Shylock's experiences as portrayed in the play.

(a) He has loaned money to Bassanio with Antonio as the guarantor of the loan. Shylock wants to have nothing to do with Antonio, who has treated Shylock detestably:

> He hath disgraced me and
> hindered me half a million, laughed at my losses,
> mocked at my gains, scorned my nation, thwarted
> my bargains, cooled my friends, heated mine enemies;
> and what's his reason? I am a Jew. (III.1.53–7)

Finally, however, he agrees to loan Antonio the 3,000 ducats without interest, only requiring that if Antonio should prove unable to repay the debt by the specified date three months hence, he must surrender a pound of his flesh.

(b) When Antonio can't pay, Shylock takes him to court and demands his pound of flesh. Bassanio's new wife Portia disguises herself as a male attorney and first offers Shylock 9,000 ducats in place of the pound of flesh, but Shylock refuses. Portia urges mercy (IV.1.190–211) – this is the focus of Derrida's commentary (Derrida 1999: 30–45; Venuti 2001b: 183–97) – and backs her urging with money (she's rich); but Shylock remains adamant. For him it's not about the money, or the letter of the law: he hates Antonio for his smug anti-Semitism and wants to make him suffer. It's an affair of the heart. It's blood revenge.

(c) As Shylock is about to begin cutting Antonio's flesh ("nearest his heart": IV.1.265), Portia launches two powerful legal quibbles (clinging casuistically to

---

[15] I repeat: what exactly is the relevance of this bison story? [Tr]

the letter of the law): (1) the bond only allows Shylock to remove flesh, not blood; if he sheds one drop of Antonio's blood, Venetian law requires that all his assets be stripped from him by the state. And (2) he must cut out exactly one pound: "if the scale do turn / But in the estimation of a hair, / Thou diest, and all thy goods are confiscate" (IV.1.344–46).

(d) Beaten, Shylock reluctantly gives up the pound-of-flesh plan and asks for the 9,000 ducats Portia offered him earlier, but she says (still clinging tenaciously to the letter of the law) that he has already rejected that offer in court.

(e) Portia next invokes a Venetian law prescribing that any alien (and a Jew is an "alien" by default)[16] who tries to take the life of a Venetian citizen must forfeit all his property, half to the intended victim (Antonio), the other half to the state; and the duke may decide whether to have Shylock executed or spare his life. Shylock asks to be executed, because if all his assets are confiscated he will have no way to make a living.

(f) The duke spares Shylock's life, but in return requires that Shylock convert to Christianity and deed all his assets to his alienated daughter Jessica and her Christian intended, Lorenzo. If Shylock refuses this offer, he will be executed. He agrees.

In summary, then, in (c–f) the Christians threaten to kill Shylock unless he gives up all his assets and converts to Christianity. Let us consider reading this as an anticipation of the Holocaust: four centuries later, six million Shylocks are killed and their assets are seized by the state. To avoid this fate, some Jews convert to Christianity, but that doesn't save their lives or their assets. (To the Nazis Judaism was not a religion but a biological race, a blood inheritance. They could not trade it away by converting.)

And in (a–c), imagine the grisly business of exacting a pound of flesh in lieu of a repayment of debt as an anticipation of zombies eating human flesh. Back in Act III Salarino said, "Why, I am sure if he forfeit, thou wilt not take his flesh! What's that good for?" and Shylock replied, "To bait fish withal; if it will feed nothing else, it will feed my revenge" (III.1.50–3).

It is but a small escalation of that revenge from an affect to a hungry subrational revenant.

Not, I might add, to an imagined European bison.

---

[16] Shylock refers three times to his "nation," once calling it "sacred" (I.3.41, III.1.52, III.1.83). As we've seen in "Six Million Shylocks: A Zombie Memoir," Part 1.1, Venetian Jews in those days were confined to the Campo di Ghetto Nuovo, "camp of the new ghetto"; the point now is that they referred to the three ethnic groups – the Ashkenazim (Germans and Italians), the Levantines (Middle Easterners), and the Ponentines (Spaniards and Portuguese) – as "nations." Shakespeare doesn't specify to which nation Shylock belonged; the main point is that members of all three "nations" were by definition aliens in Venice. [Au]

Six Million Shylocks: A Zombie Memoir, Part 3.3
By Jacques Derrida
Pseudotranslated by Douglas Robinson

That strange exchange was followed by a long uneasy wait, while we sat listening on edge to the crashes and thrashes within.

Finally:

"There is," one man said, with a quick glance over at Rabbi Abravanel, "a secret passageway behind that wall. Built centuries ago, when it was important to have access to a quick and easy escape route. One that pursuers would not identify as a door."

"But apparently," I ventured, "not quite kept clear of debris for easy access?"

"Unfortunately," the man said, "you're right."

Now the wall opened up, and what stepped out into the room was not a bison, certainly not a hinny or a zedonk, but an old Jewish man in a black gaberdine cloak, wearing a yellow cap.

We all caught our breaths. Not quite a gasp.

Some of us, I'm sure of it, were still half-expecting a European bison.

The old man walked disjointedly. His elbows and knees bent at erratic angles. His hands, and sometimes his left foot, described disastrous arcs. The man's eyes were dead. Almost as black as his cloak.

The man in the black cloak stopped, noticed us. He stood for a long minute, looking without looking – certainly without turning his head to scan the room with those black eyeballs.

Then he opened his mouth. At first no sound came out. Finally he said "Ahhhhhh . . . "

No one in the room said a word. All eyes were on him.

He took a step toward the door. Then another step. He moved stiffly, awkwardly. As if about to topple over, collapse, with every step.

He said "Ahhh . . . " again.

Gradually he managed to stagger and shuffle his way over to the door that gave out onto the square. The young woman standing there shrank back out of his way, pressing herself into a dark corner. He lifted his right arm, slowly, deliberately, as if having to plan his motions in advance. Finally he managed to seize the door handle and open the door. He stumbled out.

3.4 Mercy and Revenge: Spirit and Body

In (b) and at various other points along the way Portia and the duke urge Shylock to show mercy, which they specifically espouse as a spiritual virtue that stands in stark contrast to Shylock's vindictive obsession with the flesh. Derrida keeps returning to this body–spirit dualism in the Christian imagination of Judaism:

> This impossible translation, this conversion (and all translation is a conversion: *vertere, transvertere, convertere*, as Cicero said) between the original, literal flesh and the monetary sign[17] is not unrelated to the Jew Shylock's forced conversion to Christianity, since the traditional figure of the Jew is often and conventionally situated on the side of the body and the letter (from bodily circumcision or Pharisaism, from ritual compliance to literal exteriority), whereas St. Paul the Christian is on the side of the spirit or sense, of interiority, of spiritual circumcision. This relation of the letter to the spirit, of the body of literalness to the ideal interiority of sense is also the site of the passage of translation, of this conversion that is called translation. (Venuti 2001b: 184)

> She [Portia] tries to convert him to Christianity by persuading him of the supposedly Christian interpretation that consists of interiorizing, spiritualizing, idealizing what among Jews (it is often said, at least, that this is a very powerful stereotype) will remain physical, external, literal, devoted to a respect for the letter. (194)

Zombies too, of course, are paradigmatically all body and no spirit. (Except for Melanie, the eponymous protagonist of *The Girl with All the Gifts*, discussed in Section 4b. She is a second-generation zombie born with spirit intact – and it's a Nazi spirit. Portia rediviva.)

---

[17] For a detailed unpacking of this "impossible translation" in Nietzsche's *Genealogy*, see my *Exorcizing Translation* (Robinson 2017: 76–82). According to Nietzsche, in fact, the "impossible translation" (96) between flesh and money was rendered entirely possible by legislation: the creditor "could cut out an amount of flesh proportionate to the amount of the debt, and we find, very early, quite detailed legal assessments of the value of individual parts of the body" (Golffing 1956: 196). In translation studies, as Anthony Pym (2010: 6) reminds us, this is called "equivalence": not identity but equal value. Applying that distinction to Derrida's mapping of translation might give us "impossible translation" requiring identity-in-kind and "most possible translation" or "relevant translation" requiring equivalence – or, in his terms, what is "appropriate, pertinent, adequate, opportune, pointed, univocal, idiomatic" (Venuti 2001b: 177). Gideon Toury's (2012) "assumed equivalence" and Theo Hermans' (2014: 6) "equivalence is proclaimed, not found" would arguably solve Derrida's problem equally well. And as Nietzsche reminds us, just as there are workarounds for the nonexistence of perfect synonymy within or between languages, so too have there been historical workarounds for the nonexistence of perfect punitive equivalence between flesh and money. If Derrida had remembered that passage in Nietzsche, he might not have called the translation between flesh and money "impossible," but lumped it in with more conventionally textual forms of "relevant translation." [Au]

Derrida neglects to mention in connection with "St. Paul the Christian [being] *on the side of* the spirit or sense" that Paul's side-taking links body or letter to *killing*: God "also hath made us able ministers of the new testament," Paul writes to the Corinthians; "not of the letter, but of the spirit: for the letter killeth, but the spirit giveth life" (2 Cor. 3:6, KJV). The letter is the body of the text; in the court scenes in *The Merchant of Venice*, it is specifically the letter of the law. Shylock invokes the letter of the *bond* signed by Antonio to demand his pound of flesh, which would likely kill him; Portia invokes the letter of Venetian law to strip Shylock of all his assets and threatens to have him killed if he fails to surrender his possessions.

The Christian side famously thematizes the standoff in binary terms: the Jew invokes the letter that killeth (revenge); the Christian invokes the spirit that giveth life (mercy). But actually, that self-congratulatory Christian binary to the contrary, *both* sides invoke the letter of the law in order to kill. The Christian invocation of the spirit that giveth life levies a carceral penalty that is nakedly and unashamedly enforced by the letter that killeth. All the "spiritual" talk of mercy and forgiveness is theological gaslighting. It is demanded of the Jews, not offered by the Christians.

And we have already seen Derrida's carefully controlled Jewish ire at the merciless Christian destruction of Shylock in the name of mercy: "No one could better express the 'mercenary' dimension of 'merci' in every sense of this word. And no one could ever express it better than Shakespeare, who has been charged with anti-Semitism for a work that stages with an unequalled power all the great motives of Christian anti-Judaism" (Venuti 2001b: 191).[18] Fictional Holocaust zombies (and golems) have explicitly been mobilized by post-World War II storytellers in the service of revenge against those "great motives of Christian anti-Judaism" – and, well, by "Jacques Derrida" (that Algerian Jewish heteronym) in "his" zombie memoir.

Six Million Shylocks: A Zombie Memoir, Part 3.4
By Jacques Derrida
Pseudotranslated by Douglas Robinson

---

[18] Batchelor (2023: 10) tracks how Derrida "contrasts the divine grandeur of forgiveness with the cynical human calculations that hide behind it, foregrounding Shylock's perspective. Anchored in Derrida's own Jewishness and in which his irritation at Portia's logic is strongly evident, this reading centres on Portia's declaration, 'Then must the Jew be merciful'." She also notes that Hélène Cixous (Milesi 2012) refers to this section as an "immense, painful parenthesis" – painful because Cixous sees Derrida "analys[ing] in the most powerful [but also carefully restrained] way *bad faith* in the *use of* Christian *faith* and the theme of pardon misappropriated by a cunning which finds in Portia Shakespeare [*sic*] its first and last mouthpiece." See also Footnote 5 for a discussion of Bolduc's (2023) reading of mercy/*merci* and "the Jewish question" as the thematic core of Derrida's essay. [Au]

"Does . . . " I began, and stopped, uncertain. All eyes turned to me. "Does anyone know who that was?"

No one answered.

"I guess not?" I hazarded.

"He was dressed," said Rabbi Abravanel slowly, "like the Jewish residents of the Ghetto in the sixteenth and seventeenth centuries."

"Oh?"

"Yes. The black gaberdine cloak and the yellow cap. Jews elsewhere in Italy had to wear a badge with a yellow O on their clothing. Here we were required to wear that yellow cap."

"We": spoken not as someone who was alive then, but as someone who spoke for the entire Venetian Jewish community.

"Interesting," I said. "Perhaps he had dressed up early for Carnival?"

4 A Short History of Holocaust Zombies

Most of us know the zombie origin stories. In Haitian folklore, where the name comes from, zombies are dead bodies brought back to life, typically through Vodou magic; in George A. Romero's 1968 movie *Night of the Living Dead* they were called ghouls, but fans renamed them zombies; the meme of zombies eating brains came from later zombie movies like *Dawn of the Living Dead* (1978) and *The Return of the Living Dead* (1985).

In this section, however, I zero in on a narrower subgenre of zombie stories, following a useful three-part series in Medium.com by Elana Gomel (2024) titled "Corpses of Memory: Holocaust Zombies."

4.1 The Theory

Gomel begins by airing the shock some people feel at seeing Holocaust zombies in novels, movies, and video games,[19] and their strong disapproval at the "cheapening" or "degrading" effect these images might have on memories of the suffering of six million Jews. Her response:

> Yes, Holocaust zombies are shocking. But this is why we need them: to bring back the visceral, corporeal memory of the atrocity that the Nazi genocide of Jews actually was. The monstrous body of the Holocaust zombie breaks through the proliferating historical and pseudo-historical narratives that disguise, obscure, or falsify the reality of the genocidal violence of the Holocaust. History consoles. Memory brings back the trauma of reality. And where the Holocaust is concerned, this is a good thing.

Not just "memory" but memories: "visceral, corporeal memories"; the "monstrous bodies" of memories. They *return* to bring back "the trauma of reality." Not what Derrida calls "what, in being freed from the body, is elevated above it, interiorizes it, spiritualizes it, preserves it in memory" (Venuti 2001b: 199), but the uncanny repetition compulsions of "haunting bodies" that arise like the "something" that "seems to work against" the Hegelian dialectics, that

---

[19] Gomel does not discuss the movies or the video games, but she does list some titles featuring Holocaust zombies: video games like *Call of Duty* and movies like *Dead Snow, Overlord,* and *Frankenstein's Army.* [Au]

"secretly, silently, and insistently undermines and reworks them from the inside out" (Levine 2022).

Translation as that embodied memory, that bodily transfer of past trauma into the present.

Gomel writes about the "crisis" of narrative historiography, as meaningful links become harder and even almost impossible to maintain between a horrific past and the "political free-for-all" that the present has become, "littered with what Han [Byung-Chul] calls 'junk-shops – great dumps of images of all kinds and origins, used and shop-soiled symbols' (Han 2024: 39)." "Unfortunately," she adds, "the Holocaust has become part of the 'junk-shop' of atrocity instead of a unique historical event that it was." She paraphrases Lawrence Langer (1995: 7) as suggesting that "collective trauma expresses itself through phantasmagoric eruption of the past into the present" and adds: "Trauma is the past repeating itself in the present in all its irreducible violence, beyond ideological falsehoods or convenient excuses. Trauma is the body of the victim that refuses to stay buried."

And so:

> Zombies are monsters of repetition. They die, rise, eat the living who die, rise again ... rinse and repeat. And they are also monsters of body horror: decaying but alive; rotting but unburied; mindless but persistent. Zombies are a fantastic reflection of what inmates in Nazi camps called the *Muselmänner*: those prisoners whose emaciation and degradation made them into "mummy-men, the living dead" (Primo Levi; qtd in Stratton 2017, 262). The *Muselmann* was the "figure that assaulted the memory of those who survived the concentration camps ... It named the final stages of the condition of 'utmost inanition', beyond starvation, beyond life, beyond reason, indifferent to pain and suffering, utterly abject and scorned but not yet dead" (Luckhurst 2016, 113). (Gomel 2024)

Of course Shylock is not a *Muselmann*. But throughout the court scene in Act IV he certainly becomes more and more abject, more lost and confused in his abjection.

Six Million Shylocks: A Zombie Memoir, Part 4.1
By Jacques Derrida
Pseudotranslated by Douglas Robinson

"He, um," the young woman huddled into the dark corner under the window said. All eyes turned to her. "He dropped something. A wadded-up piece of paper, it looked like."

No one moved. Finally she stood and walked over to the door, bent down to pick something up off the floor.

It was indeed a crumpled scrap of paper, torn, with ragged edges. She straightened it out, cleared her throat.

At first she could not find her voice. She swallowed hard three or four times.

"It says, in English," she said finally, her cheeks glowing red, "'Do I not bleed?'"

4.2 Female Zombies

By Holocaust zombies Gomel means both Jewish zombies and Nazi zombies. Sometimes, as in John Blackburn's (1958/1961) novel *A Scent of New-Mown Hay* or M. R. Carey's more recent *The Girl with All the Gifts* (2014), the zombies are neither undead Jews nor undead Nazis, but women infected with a fungus created by a surviving (or zombified) female Nazi. In Blackburn's novel the infection is a surviving female doctor's revenge for the crushing of Nazism in World War II; in Carey's, however, the "girl with all the gifts" from the title is Melanie, a second-generation zombie who retains her intelligence – her "spirit" – and uses it to release the fungus into the world, with the Nazi utopian plan of purifying the human race.

In another recent female zombie story the zombie is Jewish. John Ajvide Lindqvist is a Swedish horror writer; his 2021 short story "She" tells the tale of a Swedish couple who hire a Polish construction firm to build them a house for a lot less money than a Swedish firm would have charged. Once they move in, however, they are awakened by a horrible crashing noise and find a woman's body tumbling down from the attic at the end of a hangman's noose. This is not a ghost; her body is physically palpable. "Her head jerked forward and her hair fell over her face, and at the same time, I heard a sort of wet, dull crack like breaking ice" (Lindqvist 2023: 20). The couple wakes the next morning to find the body gone, but the hanging scene is repeated the next night, and the next, until at the end of the story we find the couple hiding out in their bedroom as a zombie slouches like some rough beast toward their door:

> We heard a dragging noise from the corridor, flowed by a series of wet crunches, like when a chiropractor adjusts your joints.
> There was silence for a few seconds, then we heard what we feared most of all. Footsteps. Approaching the bedroom door.
> What do the dead want of the living?
> We would soon find out. (44)

What the dead want, Gomel suggests, is "to be let in."

It turns out that the Polish construction firm built their house out of a big old tree that had been used as a hanging tree in World War II. The hanging in the Swedish couple's house was a reenactment of a scene from the war, in which the Nazis murdered the entire population of a small Jewish village. One girl tried to run but was brought down by a bullet from a Swedish sniper and then hanged from that tree. The Swedish sniper was the grandfather of the husband, the story's first-person narrator; and it was with the money willed to the couple by the grandfather that they paid for the house.

As Gomel tells the story, "This history is not known by the characters in the story because they do not want to know." Nobody wants to know. The grandfather and the other principals in the story are all dead. And, as Gomel adds, "The dead are forgotten. Until they return." She sums up the story:

> The Jewish girl's "bare life," perpetually dying but never quite dead, brings back the past not as a story told and dispensed with but as a trauma repeating itself through generations. The compulsion of the dead to mingle with the living is summed up in the last line of the story: "It's not that easy to escape the past" (44). The past is not the weaselly words on paper or computer screen. The past is the tortured Jewish body being hanged again, and again, and again – neither dead nor alive but caught up in the limbo of memory.

Six Million Shylocks: A Zombie Memoir, Part 4.2
By Jacques Derrida
Pseudotranslated by Douglas Robinson

Fierce whispering, as people turned to their neighbors to ask what the four words the young woman had read meant.

"Can anyone interpret the message?" Rabbi Abravanel asked the crowd.

"Um, I think I can," I said.

"Yes?"

I had an odd disproportionate feeling of – well, I confess it: of greatness. Almost heroism. *I had read the Shakespeare. I was giving a seminar on the Shakespeare.*

Absurd, of course.

I smiled.

4.3 Jewish Zombies

The published Holocaust zombie tale that best lends itself to the imaginary sequelization of *The Merchant of Venice*, however, is a 2012 Polish novel, Igor Ostachowicz's (2012) *Noc żywych Żydów* ("Night of the Living Jews"),[20] in which the Jews murdered in Poland during World War II are reanimated and rise

---

[20] The novel has not yet been translated into English; for a Spanish translation, see Villaverde (2014); for a French translation, see Jannès-Kalinowski (2016).

as zombies from basements and unmarked graves. As Jan Borowicz (2015) reports, "The explicit justification for their appearance given by *Night of the Living Jews* is simple: Jewish victims of the Holocaust and World War II have been forgotten" (176). The novel has been surprisingly popular in Poland, but also, as one might expect, politically controversial. "Ultimately," Gomel (2024) sums up the debates, "the novel is not a resolution but a symptom of the very problem it tries to address: the chasm between (narrative) history and (traumatic) memory." Specifically, that means that "the undead Jews function not as an attempt to create an alternative (more truthful or more complete) narrative of the Holocaust in Poland but rather as a mute and bewildering witness to what such a narrative would both reveal and conceal: millions of corpses, left either unburied or un-mourned or both."

"Millions of corpses": "Jacques Derrida's" "zombie memoir" interwoven with this long essay, "Six Million Shylocks," shifts the scene of this million-headed return from Poland and the Holocaust to Venice, as a zombie sequel to Shakespeare's play. The zombie Shylocks return with a redoubled determination to get their pound of flesh – *exactly* that pound's worth – out of every Gentile body they encounter. And eat it. And turn their Portian tormentors into zombies like them.

Six Million Shylocks: A Zombie Memoir, Part 4.3
By Jacques Derrida
Pseudotranslated by Douglas Robinson

"It is from William Shakespeare's play about Shylock, the Venetian Jew. *The Merchant of Venice*. Written in the late sixteenth century. Shylock," I added, "would have lived here, in the Ghetto Nuovo."

"Of course," Rabbi Abravanel murmured.

"Actually," I added, "the full context goes like this: 'If you prick us, do we not bleed? If you tickle us, do we not laugh? If you poison us, do we not die? And if you wrong us, shall we not revenge?'"

"I know the passage in Ladino," Rabbi Abravanel said, and recited it.

Nods all around. One man started to applaud; stopped himself mid-clap. He looked around him in mild apologetic embarrassment, murmuring "*scusi, scusi ...*"

"So," I said, "a tall man, shall we assume a tall Jewish man? Dressed up in sixteenth-century Jewish garb, carrying a scrap of paper loosely tying him to Shakespeare's Shylock, or to the Venetian Jews to whom Shylock was referring en masse. What shall we conclude?"

5 Toward a Zombie Ecology of (Un)translatability

5.1 The Philosophical Zombie

That famous monologue that Shylock delivers in *The Merchant of Venice* more fully goes like this:

> I am a Jew. Hath not a Jew eyes? Hath not a Jew hands, organs, dimensions, senses, affections, passions? Fed with the same food, hurt with the same weapons, subject to the same diseases, healed by the same means, warmed and cooled by the same winter and summer, as a Christian is? If you prick us, do we not bleed? If you tickle us, do we not laugh? If you poison us, do we not die? And if you wrong us, shall we not revenge? If we are like you in the rest, we will resemble you in that. If a Jew wrong a Christian, what is his humility? Revenge. If a Christian wrong a Jew, what should his sufferance be by Christian example? Why, revenge. The villainy you teach me, I will execute, and it shall go hard but I will better the instruction. (III.1.57–72)

In analytic philosophy since Otto Neurath and Rudolf Carnap in the 1930s, physicalism – these days reportedly the majority view among analytic philosophers – is the belief that there is nothing that is not physical. Everything is physical. There is only one substance in the universe: physicality (i.e., material monism). That means that if there is such a thing as mind, or consciousness, or subjectivity, or qualia, it/they must be an entirely physical thing, or at least have an entirely physical cause. (This extension is called the "causal closure of physics.") If those mental experiences are not reducible to physicality, they simply do not exist. If I tell you what it feels like to be me, and you tell me what it feels like to be you, and we find significant differences between the two but also some common ground, either we are deluded in thinking that we have such experiences, or those experiences must be reducible to physical causes.

Saul Kripke (1972/1980: 153ff) famously posed this hypothetical: if God had created the world with the idea of creating a purely physical universe, and, once he'd finished that, started thinking that he really needed to provide for consciousness, would that have required more work, or not? Physicalists would say no: creating the physical world would be enough to create any thoughts, feelings, experiences, and so forth that people might claim to possess. Antiphysicalists would say yes, it would have required more work: the physical facts alone cannot explain consciousness. Consciousness depends on at least some nonphysical properties.

In Shylock's monologue at the beginning of this section, obviously the eyes, hands, organs, dimensions (the human shape and form), and senses are physiological things. But what about Shylock using his eyes and ears and nose to enjoy the calm beauty of a spring day? Is that purely physical? What about Shylock's feeling of running his hands over a cat's fur, or a tree trunk, or (in memory) his deceased wife Leah's bare skin? Is that purely physical? And what about affections and passions? To the physicalist they must be treated as neural activity, synaptic transmissions. To the extent that we map those transmissions mentally, and say that we "feel" affections or passions, and assume that our feelings are qualitatively different from the physical causes of those things, the physicalists say we are deluded. For the physicalist, being "hurt with the same weapons" must mean physical injuries only – not the feeling of pain, and certainly not emotional injury. If you prick us, yes, we bleed – but we don't feel pain. If you tickle us, we laugh, but that is purely an autonomic response to physical pressure on the ribs or skin. We don't feel hilarity.

And what about feeling wronged and lusting for revenge? Not physical: not real.

What makes this strain of analytical philosophy relevant to revenant translation is that antiphysicalists like David Chalmers (1996: 94–106) have developed the notion of a "philosophical zombie," or "p-zombie," as a thought experiment designed to disprove physicalism. A p-zombie is thought to be physically identical to a neurotypical but completely lacking in conscious experience:

> What is going on in my zombie twin? He is physically identical to me, and we may as well suppose that he is embedded in an identical environment. He will certainly be identical to me functionally: he will be processing the same sort of information, reacting in a similar way to inputs, with his internal configurations being modified appropriately and with indistinguishable behavior resulting. He will be psychologically identical to me, in the sense developed in Chapter 1. He will be perceiving the trees outside, in the functional sense, and tasting the chocolate, in the psychological sense. All of this follows logically from the fact that he is physically identical to me, by virtue of the functional analyses of psychological notions. He will even be "conscious" in the functional senses described earlier – he will be awake, able to report the contents of his internal states, able to focus attention in various places, and so on. It is just that none of this functioning will be accompanied by any real conscious experience. There will be no phenomenal feel. There is nothing it is like to be a zombie. (95)

Chalmers notes that the zombies he is imagining are not like "Hollywood zombies" – the kind based since 1968 on George Romero's *Night of the Living Dead*. "Typically," he notes, those zombies have "little capacity for introspection and lack a refined ability to voluntarily control behavior" (95). Ned Block (1995) suggests that "it is reasonable to suppose that there is something it tastes like when they eat their victims" (quoted in Chalmers 1996: 95). Chalmers calls those other zombies "psychological zombies," and says he is imagining "phenomenal zombies," in the sense that they *lack* phenomenality – the ability to feel themselves living, feel themselves experiencing. They might see the colors of that spring day, hear the sounds, smell the smells, but they don't realize they are perceiving those things, and can't enjoy them.

In a sense the Shylocks in "Six Million Shylocks" are p-zombies. They behave like the George Romero zombies that have dominated zombie movies and fictions since 1968: they stagger disjointedly, they have dead eyes, they can't talk, and, since *Dawn of the Living Dead* in 1978, they eat brains. But at one point, when the Portia Brigade has taken up positions around the perimeter and are machine-gunning the Shylocks down, the Shylocks stop staggering stupidly forward and turn back, ducking into the secret passageways that allow them to come up behind the Portias' positions around the perimeters and kill them. They behave as if they have the mental ability to think strategically, to make and carry out a military plan to outflank and decimate the enemy. They can't talk; their eyes remain dead; to all outward appearances they are still the mindless undead bodies that zombies have been since Romero's "ghouls" in *Night of the Living Dead*. But it's difficult to imagine them outflanking the Portias without the consciousness required to make a plan.

What made me think of Shylock's monologue was that antiphysicalists have argued that if a p-zombie were pricked, it would bleed, and flinch away from the pain – but would not *feel* any pain. P-zombies are a useful test of physicalism because flinching is a physical effect, and according to the "causal closure of physics" must have a physical cause; but if we neurotypical human beings *feel the pain*, and *flinch away from the pain that we feel*, the flinching has a nonphysical cause. The injury is physical, but the pain is a quale, a qualitative experience. There is something that it's like to be in pain. We feel pain. And if the p-zombies are acting in exactly the same way normal human beings act in response to pain but are thought to have no conscious life, no way to feel the pain, we have to assume that there is some other nonphysical cause behind the flinching. (In zombie movies the "psychological zombies" typically show no fear of shotguns and the like, and do not seem to feel the pain of limbs being blown off. In that way they are clearly different from normal humans. David

Chalmers posits "phenomenal zombies" as a way of proving that antiphysicalism doesn't adequately account for human consciousness.)

Chalmers cites Block (1978) on a possible nonphysical cause like this: "the people of a large nation such as China might organize themselves so that they realize a causal organization isomorphic to that of my brain, with every person simulating the behavior of a single neuron, and with radio links corresponding to synapses. The population might control an empty shell of a robot body, equipped with sensory transducers and motor effectors" (Chalmers 1996: 97).[21] And arguably they could create a plausible simulation of consciousness. They could simulate feeling in the robot body – or the zombie.

Obviously the existence of those Chinese people is a physical fact, and the radio links involve oscillating electric and magnetic fields that push the electrons in the receiving antenna around, which creates a tiny oscillating voltage, and all that is physical. But the *simulations* are not physical. They are mental/experiential constructs based on experientially organized imitations.

Whether this is a plausible scenario, Chalmers says, is beside the point. The point is to ask whether the observed identical behaviors of a p-zombie Shylock flinching away from an injury and a neurotypical human Shylock flinching away from a feeling of pain can be plausibly assigned a physical cause. Chalmers says no. The behavioral response to an injury without a feeling of pain would be observably different from the behavioral response to pain.

He admits that there are other ways of combatting physicalism and thus underscoring what he calls "the hard problem of consciousness" (Chalmers 1996: xi–xii) – namely, that it seems to require mind–body dualism but there is no scientifically or philosophically credible explanation for the separate existence of mind. David Stoljar (2018), for example, suggests that it's enough to imagine two physically identical humans who have different tastes in coffee. That one deviation should be enough to overthrow physicalism.[22]

Still, Chalmers insists, we're so familiar with the close coexistence of biochemistry and consciousness that it's all too easy for us to assume a conceptual or even physical link. The p-zombie postulate is a useful way of highlighting the key differences.

---

[21] I'm writing this in China and trying to remember how we Westerners felt about the Chinese back in 1978. Block's image of the Chinese as numberless, faceless, identical participants in an experiment that can only simulate consciousness seems like it probably would have fit the Orientalist stereotype: the "yellow horde" as a billion identically replicable neurons. [Au]

[22] One of the reviewers of this book for the publisher suggested that a good counterargument to Stoljar's thought experiment might be that "people have different tastes for coffee because they are not actually physically identical (e.g. there might be differences within their brains or taste buds . . .)." What that shows, of course, is that the p-zombie argument is based on an extremely shaky distinction between physical identity and phenomenological difference: tweak either just slightly and the p-zombie thesis staggers. [Au]

Six Million Shylocks: A Zombie Memoir, Part 5.1
By Jacques Derrida
Pseudotranslated by Douglas Robinson

"Did anyone notice his eyes?" Rabbi Abravanel asked. "His dead eyes?" Many nodded again. "The last time I saw eyes like that was in the camps. We called them *Muselmänner*."

"You survived a concentration camp?" I asked.

"I was a survivor, yes," Rabbi Abravanel said. "In the Risiera di San Sabba in Trieste. As a very young man."

"And the *Muselmänner*," I said, "were not Muslims, if I remember correctly."

"That's right," Rabbi Abravanel said. "It was a misnomer. They were prisoners who had been utterly and irrevocably dehumanized by trauma. They were like ghouls. Like the living dead." He paused. "We have in Italy a philosopher named Giorgio Agamben. Agamben cites a law passed in the ancient Roman Empire banning from society and revoking the rights as a citizen of anyone who had committed a certain kind of crime. They called that kind of person a *homo sacer*, 'holy man.' A *homo sacer* could be killed with impunity by anyone. Under the laws of the Third Reich, all of us Jews were *homines sacri*. That status killed most of us in the gas chambers, and drove many of those who survived physically out of our minds. The *Muselmänner* were the most pathetic."

5.2 Hegelian Ghosts, Marxist Zombies

We've seen Derrida associating the Hegelian *Aufhebung/relève* with "the resurrection of the ghost or of the glorious body that rises, rises again [*se relève*] – and walks" (Venuti 2001b: 200); now it is time to remember that German Idealism, the idealism that powered Hegel's dialectics, has widely (at least until recently) been read as a monism of the spirit – the exact opposite of physicalism, a monism of the body. This reading of Hegel has met with serious challenges since the late twentieth century, for example from Robert Pippin (1989, 2010, 2019) and Terry Pinkard (1994, 2000, 2012), and, from an analytic perspective, by Robert Brandom (2002, 2014, 2019) and John McDowell (2006, 2018). Since what I want from Hegel is not the full complexity of his idealist metaphysics but a model, even a caricature that can serve as a model, I will ignore the new rethinking and outline the old reading of his idealism: the idea that the mind/spirit of God only emerges into full worldly existence by being particularized in and as the minds of humans (and the aggregate of those human minds is "spirit"). Because we humans were created by

God, we are conscious of his consciousness, and that allows us to realize his self-consciousness, which is his perfection. In this view, mind or spirit is the basis of all creation; the objective world is objectified spirit. As a result, Hegel's idealism was thought to be "objective idealism." But because Hegel combined objective idealism with the subjective idealism of individuals, he was more accurately characterized as an "Absolute Idealist," believing in God's self-consciousness and self-actualization as Absolute Spirit. The historical development of that Absolute Spirit in objective cultural practices and its psychological and intellectual development in the minds of individuals were interlinked features of his idealism.

Think of Hegel's idealism as feeding the antiphysicalism of the previous section: human beings are partially physicalized instantiations of mind or spirit. Now consider the materialist turn brought to Hegelian thought by Karl Marx: instead of starting with spirit and imagining the physical world as objectified spirit, Marx started with the material conditions under which people live and work and relegated "spirit" to the realm of illusion and distortion.

But actually it's a bit more complicated than that. If we read "spirit" as "ideology," Marx was pretty much all over the place with that notion. In some moods he described ideology as sheer gaslighting perpetrated by the ruling class, especially in feudalism and capitalism; in those moods (by which I basically mean the Marx idealized by the Second International and baked into the core state policy of the Soviet Union) his belief was that once the socialist state had taken control of the means of production, the illusions and delusions of ideology would fade away and be replaced by hardcore practical knowhow. When that didn't happen in the Soviet Union, the Bolsheviks couldn't figure out who to blame or how to begin to fix the problem. The primary solution was what Leon Trotsky called the "Thermidor" of Josef Stalin: a paranoid bureaucracy dedicated to the random arrests and executions of whole families, whole neighborhoods, whole groups of people, in the millions.

What is variously called Western Marxism or Hegelian Marxism assigned ideology a more active role in stabilizing a society. That stabilization was arguably the cause of the resistance Soviet citizens displayed to the utopian Soviet expectation of change – indeed, expectation of perfection: "Soviet Man." The reason state ownership of the means of production didn't magically transform Soviet citizens into "New" Men and Women was that the ideological "spirit" had the lingering power to condition the behavioral "body" – specifically, in this case, to condition "body" to resist pressures to change – and the state didn't recognize or understand that power.

What I want to get out of this digression, though, is a suggestion: that the Western Marxist human was a human body guided by consciousness, and the Second International Marxist(-Leninist-Stalinist) human was a p-zombie, imagined as guided entirely by physicality once the superstructural illusion of ideological consciousness had been jettisoned.

> Six Million Shylocks: A Zombie Memoir, Part 5.2
> By Jacques Derrida
> Pseudotranslated by Douglas Robinson
>
> "And our guest," I said, "who emerged mysteriously from that secret passageway, was either bare life or an uncanny imitation of bare life."
> "Yes," Rabbi Abravanel said. "And if I might speculate: either someone dressed as Shylock, with contact lenses to make his eyes look dead, or Shylock himself returned from the dead."
> A shiver went through me. It seemed to me that it went through the others as well. A thrill, almost.
> More like a shock from a frayed electric cord.

5.3 The Death of the Original and its Return as a Zombie Text

Recall now Jacques Derrida translating Walter Benjamin's *das Überleben* as *vie par-delà la mort* "life after death" (see Section 3.1): "Elle assurerait ainsi la *survie* du corps de l'original (*survie* au double sens que lui donne Benjamin dans *La Tâche du traducteur*, *fortleben* et *überleben*: vie prolongée, vie continuée, living on, mais aussi vie par-delà la mort)" (Derrida 1999: 46; Derrida's emphasis). "It would thus guarantee the *survival* of the body of the original (*survival* in the double sense that Benjamin gives it in 'The Task of the Translator,' *[das F]ortleben* and *[das Ü]berleben*: prolonged life, continuous life, living on, but also life after death") (Venuti 2001b: 199). As we've seen, that "double sens(e)" is arguably a translation error: in Benjamin it's only survival in the *single* sense of "prolonged life, continuous life, living on." A morphological translation of *das Überleben* as "overlife" or "superlife" may be more "relevant." But as I suggested earlier, Derrida's *vie par-delà la mort* might be read as his sly hinting at a *revenant* translation – and "he" has built that reading into "his" zombie memoir "Six Million Shylocks."

And note *what* is surviving in the essay about "relevant" translation: *le corps de l'original* "the *body* of the original." The body of the source text dies and returns from the dead, but only as a body – not, say, as a spirit, a ghost, or even a body with consciousness.

In other words, the body of the source text dies and returns as a zombie translation.

A metaphor? Not quite.

Benjamin (1923/1972) actually writes that "in völlig unmetaphorischer Sachlichkeit ist der Gedanke vom Leben und Fortleben der Kunstwerke zu erfassen" (11): "in fully unmetaphorical objectivity/thinginess is the thought of the life and the continuing life of art works to be grasped." For Benjamin the art work really is alive. It's not a metaphor. He doesn't explicitly say that the source text dies and is reborn as the translation, but if we follow Harry Zohn, Steven Rendall, and Jacques Derrida in reading "so ... geht die Übersetzung aus dem Original hervor. Zwar nicht aus seinem Leben so denn aus seinem ›Überleben‹" (19) as "so emanates the translation out of the original. To be sure, not so much out of its life as out of its 'afterlife'," which is to say as death and resurrection/revivification/return, that too should be grasped in fully unmetaphorical objectivity.

The only part of "the body of the source text dies and returns as a zombie translation" that might be grasped metaphorically, in a notional reconstruction/revivification of Benjamin's embodied mind, is "the body": Benjamin says nothing about the survival of the source text's *body*. That is Derrida's addition to the image. And obviously in adding "the body" to the image, Derrida also lays the groundwork for my addition of "zombie" in "as a zombie translation." Without that specification of "the body" there is no reason to assume that the revenant translation is mindless, senseless, without a "spirit" or "soul," without consciousness.

In "Six Million Shylocks" the heteronymous "Derrida" is first led to imagine his (and Walter Benjamin's) ideal translation as a golem translation; only then, gradually, as a zombie translation.

How does Benjamin imagine the unmetaphorical *life* of a text?

In the Kabbalistic framework that he learned from his friend Gershom Scholem, the actual physical work of art embodies a divine spark that was emanated into the world when the Ein Sof ("the infinite": God prior to any self-manifestation) constricted its light, creating a void and pouring the divine light of existence into it; this is called the Tzimtzum, or construction/concentration. Each divine spark, wherever it is found, is wrapped in Kelipot (also romanized Qliphoth), the "impure shells" or "husks" that cover and conceal the sparks of the holy, to protect them from evil – but according to some Kabbalists the Kelipot originate in the Sitra Achra, the demonic other side, and yet also feed off the holy, and protect the holy sparks by placing limits on their power to reveal the truth. Evil as a necessary limitation – at least for a while, until the messianic end (see Robinson 2023: 136–40).

But Benjamin's "failure" to mention the "survival of the body" that Derrida highlights is only part of the story. For Benjamin the task of the translator is to translate as literally as possible, and so to avoid conveying the "spiritual" "sense" of the source text into the target language – because only that "senseless" or "mindless" translation strategy generates enough friction between the two languages to begin to abrade the Kelipot shells. Ultimately, in some dim distant future, translations will have worn away the Kelipot shells sufficiently to release the divine spark hidden inside texts and reveal what Benjamin calls *die reine Sprache* "pure language"[23] – but in the short term, in the act of translation, for the Derridean/Benjaminian zombie Kabbalist only the source text has a "soul," that divine spark, and in creating the translation as revenant the translator should seek *not* to convey that "soul." The translation should be soulless, senseless. Its function is not to simulate or reproduce the divine spark but to liberate it from the source language – and to that end it must be a zombie text. Effectively Benjamin's call for radical literalism that despises the "sense" adumbrates Derrida's "survival of the body" without the "soul."

Over time, then – the timeless time of *Heilsgeschichte*, sacred history – zombie translationality eats the Kelipot (let's say philological) brains[24] of source languages everywhere, gradually liberating their divine spirits. (In zombie Kabbalah the mind is not a home movie shown by the brain; it does not flicker out when the brain is eaten. The brain, and the rest of the human body, is a shell that imprisons the mind. Eating the brain breaks the mind out of prison.)

What I have been construing as Benjamin's (and Derrida's) zombie Kabbalistic take on translation is actually only a slight intensification of orthodox Jewish tradition. In addressing the Christian stereotype that Jewish thought

---

[23] Benjamin (1923/1972: 19) wrote that "Jene reine Sprache, die in fremde gebannt ist, in der eigenen zu erlösen, die im Werk gefangene in der Umdichtung zu befreien, ist die Aufgabe des Übersetzers," and in interlinear box #69 of *Translation as a Form* (Robinson 2023: 164) I translated that literally as "that pure language, which in foreign spellbound is, in the own to release, the in-the-work-imprisoned in the re-poeming to free, is the task of the translator."

I'm having second thoughts about that translation now, however. *Gebannt* is cognate to English "banned," and in German it can mean banished or outlawed, or ostracized; but in magic it means immobilized or disarmed by a spell, and I followed that in rendering it "spellbound." (My paraphrase lower on that page reads "in order to release in the target language that pure language that is spellbound in the source language.") It's true that Benjamin's mystical discourse draws heavily on the language of magic; and figuratively *gebannt* can be used to mean captivated by charm, beguiled, enraptured, enthralled, and so on, and all of that seemed attractively magical to me. The problem with that whole metaphorics, though, it seems to me now, is that it is based not only on magic spells but on charm – and charm is quite far from the dull embodied evil of the Kelipot shells that keep pure language imprisoned. It now seems far more appropriate to imagine pure language imprisoned not by a spell or in a metal cage but inside a zombie's belly. The super-jailer zombie was sent by the Sitra Achra to swallow pure language so as to protect it from discovery and misuse. [Au]

[24] This sounds a bit like Haroldo de Campos's theory of transcreation as cannibalization – except that, as Vidal Claramonte and Lee (2025: 3) write, transcreational cannibalization is "understood not as mutilation, but as a symbolic act of love, an act that absorbs the virtues of a foreign body through the transfusion of blood" – and zombies mainly just mutilate. No love, no absorption of virtues, but a lot of blood. [Au]

is all body and no spirit, Derrida neglected to mention that Jewish rabbis have tended to insist that God wrote the Bible in Hebrew, and because the shape of every letter and every diacritic and every stray ink spot was written in his own hand by God, only the body of the Hebrew Bible is holy, and thus "the Bible."[25] Translations are only cribs – which is to say, zombie texts. They cannot reproduce the holiness of the source text; they can only moan about it.

> Six Million Shylocks: A Zombie Memoir, Part 5.3
> By Jacques Derrida
> Pseudotranslated by Douglas Robinson
>
> "Or," I added, "a third possibility, since Shylock is a fictional character: Perhaps it was the revenant of some other real Italian Jew on whom Shakespeare based Shylock."
>
> "Perhaps," Rabbi Abravanel agreed.

5.4 The Legend of the Septuagint as a Gateway to Christian Theology

One historical watershed for the turn Christian theology ended up taking away from ancient Hebrew thought was arguably the legend of the Septuagint, the first Greek translation of the Hebrew Bible. According to the legend, that translation was undertaken in the early third century BCE in Alexandria by seventy-two rabbis, six from each tribe of Israel, sent by Eleazar, high priest in Jerusalem during the Second Temple period, to King Ptolemy II Philadelphus at the latter's request. This legend is attributed to one "Aristeas" (see the "Letter of Aristeas" in Robinson 2014: 4–6), who claims to have been a member of the king's bodyguard when this all took place, and to have interviewed the seventy-two translators; most likely "Aristeas" was a pseudonym of the actual unknown author, probably a devout Alexandrian Jew writing in the late second century BCE.

The Jewish neo-Platonist philosopher Philo of Alexandria, writing a century later, roughly twenty years before the supposed birth of Christ, picked up the legend and further mystified it:

> Sitting here in seclusion with none present save the elements of nature, earth, water, air, heaven, the genesis of which was to be the first theme of their sacred revelation, for the laws begin with the story of the world's creation, they became as it were possessed, and, under inspiration, wrote, not each

---

[25] For this understanding of rabbinical tradition see Joseph Dan (1986), "Midrash and the Dawn of Kabbalah"; see also Robinson (1996: 66–70) for discussion. [Au]

several scribe something different, but the same word for word, as though dictated to each by an invisible prompter. (Robinson 2014: 14)

"Possessed," "under inspiration," "dictated to … by an invisible prompter": who was that prompter? By the time the Christian Church Fathers picked up the story – especially Augustine in *On Christian Doctrine* (428 CE), but anticipated by Epiphanius of Constantia in 392 CE – that prompter had become the Holy Ghost (Robinson 2014: 34). And because the Holy Ghost was reportedly dictating the Greek translation nearly three centuries before Jesus Christ was born to a virgin to save us all from sin, etc., the Septuagint Bible *superseded* the Hebrew Bible. The Hebrew Bible, after all, was written by people who didn't know Jesus. The Septuagint was the pure and perfect Word of God.

Jerome, who had learned Hebrew from a convert while both were living as hermits in the desert, scoffed at this legend. In his "Letter to Pammachius" (395 CE; Robinson 2014: 23–30) he provided a long list of errors that the Septuagint translators had made, and in *Preface to the Pentateuch* (401 CE) he wrote:

> I know not who was the first lying author to construct the seventy cells at Alexandria, in which they were separated and yet all wrote the same words, whereas Aristeas, one of the bodyguards of the said Ptolemy, and long after him Josephus have said nothing of the sort, but write that they were assembled in a single hall and conferred together, not that they prophesied. For it is one thing to be a prophet, another to be an interpreter. (Robinson 2014: 30)

We might even push this imagery further, following Walter Benjamin's Jewish mystical tradition, and imagine that every authorized translation of the Christian Bible is itself to be understood as a conscious divine spirit-entity. The entity that "is" the Christian Bible would then be the indwelling Holy Ghost – a bodiless revenant-in-advance of the dead-and-resurrected revenant Jesus Christ that stands alongside God the Father and God the Son as a "series of [three] ghosts standing in for others, for a [triune] structure of haunting without origin or end" (Levine 2022: 8–9). Christian Bible translators take the Holy Ghost into their beings, let themselves be haunted by that revenant spirit, and let the haunting guide their choice of words and phrases – and that ghostly guidance transfers the revenant spirit *into* the text.

Six Million Shylocks: A Zombie Memoir, Part 5.4
By Jacques Derrida
Pseudotranslated by Douglas Robinson

"I remember reading," I said, "that Shakespeare based *The Merchant of Venice* on a fourteenth-century collection of historical tales by Giovanni Fiorentino called *Il pecorone*, inspired by Boccaccio's *Decamerone*."

"Inspired by Boccaccio and others, I believe," another man put in. "Such as the historical facts gathered in the *Nuova cronica* by Giovanni Villani, and the lives of the saints collected in the *Legenda aurea* and the Hebrew *Mischle sendebar*."

Learned Jews, I thought, feeling very much at home. *Heimlich*, I thought in German. And outside our four walls, *das Unheimliche*.

5.5 (Un)translatability and the Recursive/Revenant Economy of Zombification

This would be the larger spirit/letter or mind/body context for translation coming out of Portia on mercy versus Shylock on revenge: because of the Jewish rabbinical insistence on the *divine body* of the sacred source text (not) returning as the (zombie) translation-which-is-not-a-translation, the Hebrew Bible is definitively untranslatable; because of the Christian insistence that the Bible is not body but mind, not letter but spirit, it is perfectly and totally translatable.

What Derrida calls the impossible ideal of perfect translation is the core myth of Christian Bible translation. What makes that impossible ideal theoretically possible and even theologically inevitable is the divine inspiration of the Holy Ghost. What Derrida calls "relevant" translation is a secularization of that Christian mythology: in it target readers are led to *trust* human sense-for-sense translations as "the *most* possible," with generous allowances for minor imperfections.

But it's actually more complicated than that. What Jerome writes in the "Letter to Pammachius" is in fact that "in translating from the Greek – except of course in the case of Holy Scripture, where even the syntax contains a mystery – I render, not word for word, but sense for sense" (Robinson 2014: 25). The idea that "even the syntax contains a mystery" is manifestly a survival of Jewish body/letter mysticism: the actual material words on the page, or the physical sounds of the words as they were read aloud, in the source-textual sequence of words in actual sentences, were the Bible's body, the Bible's letter – the letter that killeth, as Paul insisted. The "mystery" contained in the syntax was the holiness of that body, imparted to it by God when he wrote the Bible. In worrying about protecting the holiness of that divine body by translating Scripture word for word, Jerome is still very much a Jewish rabbi.

Now given that Christianity was then still in the throes of separating itself from Jewish thought, and would be for at least a millennium to come, we might plausibly write off Jerome's mysterious-syntax exception as understandable caution. His detractors are trying to brand him a heretic for daring to translate sense for sense *a bishop's letter*. That seems harmless enough – but still potentially heretical. So now to defend himself against those heresy charges

Jerome thinks it's a good idea to write a long open letter in which he vituperously defends sense-for-sense translation of the Bible by citing all manner of translation *errors* from the Hebrew to the Greek made by the Seventy and the four Evangelists and *calling* those errors "sense-for-sense translation."

That would suggest that Jerome the eremite didn't have a tiny fraction of Augustine's institutional savvy. He had anger-management problems. He flew off the handle, and endangered himself and others.

Still, giving him the benefit of the doubt, we might imagine him starting to wonder while writing the Letter to Pammachius whether maybe attacking the Septuagint and the Greek New Testament as error-ridden wasn't necessarily the smartest move for him to be making. Better play it safe, maybe, by also claiming to translate Scripture word for word? And throw in some verbiage about "mysteries" for good measure?

But deeper analysis would suggest that "even the syntax contains a mystery" was not just a kneejerk self-protective move on Jerome's part. It wasn't an accident. It was actually the secret key to the theological shift. The Christian Church *needed* the mystery. Theologically speaking, sense-for-sense translation was a red herring.

Not only that: ultimately *all talk of translation strategies of any sort* was a red herring, a gaslighting, a spinning of theological wheels. Ultimately it didn't matter how a Bible was translated. All that mattered was winning ecclesiastical approval. If the Church approved it, it was *declared* divinely inspired. As Theo Hermans (2014) puts it, "in a particular institutional context" – Western Christian/Mormon theocratic – equivalence is not so much "extracted from texts" as it is "imposed on them through an external intervention. In other words," he adds, "equivalence is proclaimed, not found" (6).

The real shift from Jewish Bible translation theory to Christian Bible translation theory wasn't from word-for-word to sense-for-sense, or even from Holy Untranslatability to Total Translatability. It was from the divine inspiration of the *source* text to the divine inspiration of the *target* text.

The Jewish view was that the Hebrew source text was untranslatable because human translators lacked the "mysterious" ability to transfer the divine spark to a target language. The Christian answer to that was Philo's "invisible prompter," retheologized as the Holy Ghost: if human translators were incapable of transferring the divine spark to a target language, the Holy Ghost did have the spark, and indeed in some sense *was* the spark.[26] The whole idea occurred to the early

---

[26] An interesting comparison: most English translations of 2 Timothy 3:16 tell us that Scripture was *inspired* by God; the *Complete* Jewish *Bible* renders that "all Scripture is God-breathed." (Thanks to Kathryn Batchelor for directing my attention to this passage.) Most people know that *inspiration* comes from the Latin *in* + *spīrō* ("in-breathe"), but the Latin roots help abstract

Church Fathers as they read Philo[27] on the legend of the Septuagint: the Holy Ghost had the magical/mysterious power to transform a dead book (the Hebrew Bible, written by people who didn't know Jesus, which was also, by the bye, written in a language that most of the Church Fathers could not read) into a Holy Scripture (a Greek book that the Latin-speaking Church Fathers could read much better than they could the Hebrew).

Six Million Shylocks: A Zombie Memoir, Part 5.5
By Jacques Derrida
Pseudotranslated by Douglas Robinson

"If, um, if you don't mind . . . "

It was the young woman who had found the scrap of paper. She was standing at the door that gave out onto the square. "You might," she said, urgency tugging at her voice, "want to come look out here."

No one rushed to look. People stood slowly, singly and in pairs, stretched, looked over at the door, and gradually, sedately, began to make their way along the rows.

We couldn't all gather around that door. Some looked out the windows, and their eyes went wide. In the end we all stepped out onto the square – and gasped at what we saw.

The square was full of bare life – *homines sacri* in black gaberdines and yellow caps. Hundreds of *Muselmänner*, lurching and staggering across the square, heading for the bridges that would take them out of the Campo di Ghetto Nuovo and into the Christian parts of the city, on the main island and the other islands, Murano, the Lido, and the rest.

And they kept coming. They poured out of the buildings around the square like a flock of yellow-headed blackbirds, in the thousands now, perhaps tens of thousands, shuffling awkwardly in all directions. The residents of the Ghetto stood around the square, gaping at the scene.

Then – a ghastly moment. A family of Gentile tourists stood in a small grouping twenty or thirty meters from where we stood outside the synagogue, videoing the black-cloaked *Muselmänner* on the square with their

---

the breathing into a purely "spiritual" (nonphysical) event; the Jewish Bible's use of the Anglo-Saxon word "breath" encourages us to imagine God with a humanoid body, with lungs and a mouth, and a blood circulation system that needed oxygenation. In one mystical imagery God's breath is the Holy Spirit (from Latin *spīritus* "breath"), and it's the Holy Spirit that breathes life into Immaculately Conceived Zygote Jesus as a human. [Au]

[27] It was Philo's neo-Platonist *Logos*-mysticism that inspired the opening of John's Gospel: "In the beginning was the Word, and the Word was with God, and the Word was God" (John 1.1, KJV). In *Translation as a Form* (Robinson 2023: 142–44) I argue that Walter Benjamin's (1923/1972: 18) citation of that line from John is actually an allusion to Philo's Jewish *Logos*-mysticism: the *Logos* is a divine being, God's agent on earth, in whom all of the Platonic Forms dwell. [Au]

phones. Suddenly eight or ten of the black-clad *homines sacri* fell on them, and in short order killed them and started eating their flesh.

Many of our party cried out in horror and turned away. Several vomited onto the cobblestones.

Rabbi Abravanel caught my eye.

"Not *Muselmänner*," he murmured. "I said it before: zombies."

"Jewish zombies," I said. "Notice that they are not harming the Jewish residents of the Ghetto. Only the tourists."

He nodded. "This means trouble."

The young woman who had led us outside stepped up then, with her phone in hand. She showed us the videos that were already being uploaded to the Internet: a long line of Shylocks walking across the SR11 bridge to San Giuliano on the mainland, blocking traffic, some of them pushing cars over the railings into the lagoon; great masses of black-garbed Shylocks falling on the tourists in St. Mark's Square and eating them; Shylocks occupying the four main bridges, the Rialto, the Accademia, the Scalzi, and the Constitution, eating the brains of the tourists they caught and dropping the bloody corpses on the gondoliers frantically trying to pole their gondolas and clients to safety . . .

"The authorities," she said, "are already calling this 'The Night of the Jewish Undead' and 'The Shylock Invasion.'"

Rabbi Abravanel stood there with a rictus of dread. "My God," he said.

5.6 Zombie Translation as That Dangerous Ordeal

What we might call the Christian "mystery religion" began to wane in the early-modern period, under the onslaught of the pragmatism of the emergent (and mostly Protestant) middle classes.

Erasmus of Rotterdam, bastard son of a Catholic priest and his housekeeper, remained a Catholic but was a true Renaissance Humanist, and in 1516 not only retranslated the New Testament into Latin (superseding Jerome's "divinely inspired" Vulgate) but submitted the Greek source text to modern – "scientific," post-magical – text-critical analysis (see his "Letter to Maarten Lips," Robinson 2014: 65–75). His text-critical innovations were extremely influential with theologians of both the Protestant and the Catholic Reformations.

Martin Luther's German translation of the Bible appeared between 1517 and 1522; eight years later, in 1530, he defended himself against his many detractors through an attack on Jerome's Vulgate as a mystified word-for-word translation. Luther's basic method was German peasant-becoming-bourgeois common sense: you have to watch how German speakers' mouths move as they talk and translate that way (see Robinson 2014: 84–89).

William Tyndale published his English translation of the New Testament in 1526; he was arrested in 1535 and executed by the Inquisition in 1536; but by the end of that decade there were already four translations of the full Bible into English, all following Tyndale's innovations. In 1534 Henry VIII's Act of Supremacy had declared him Supreme Head of the Church of England, eventually making it safe to publish English Bibles in England.

And yet even in 1528–29, just a handful of years before refusing to swear fealty to King Henry as head of the Anglican Church (and being executed for his stubbornness), the great Catholic "Humanist" Thomas More published a fictional dialogue with a Lutheran, attacking the Protestant idea of making the Bible available to the masses in English on the grounds that then laypeople would be treating of "the mysteries of Jesus Christ" at the pub over a pint (Robinson 2014: 81).

So yes, in the early modern period Jerome's call for sense-for-sense translation (of secular texts) began to catch on, with dull civilizational memories of the Christian association of "sense" with "spirit" fueling the change. In effect what Derrida calls "relevant translations" were secularized and pragmatized early-modern descendants of magical Christian "Total Translatability."

Derrida's (Jewish?) resistance to that Christian theological history, as we saw in Section 2.1, was to subject the pressure he felt to create "relevant" translations to the "test" or "trial" or "ordeal" of the untranslatable (*l'épreuve de l'intraduisible*). In the terms I've been developing over the last few subsections, he didn't want to abstract the body of the original out of existence: he wanted that body to survive in some form, to some degree. He didn't want translation to entail the resurrection of a *ghost*, say a disembodied revenant Holy Ghost. Nor did he want his choices guided by lingering phantomatic traces of that ghost, with its power not only to dwell inside the source text and render it spiritual/semantic/relevant through and through, but to make the jump to the target text as well. *He wanted to zombify the translation.* He wanted to retain something of the mindless corporeality of untranslatability even in translation.

The recursive/revenant economy of that zombification would go something like this.

Untranslatability is translatability's dangerous supplement. It moves through the secret underground passageways below and beyond translatability like the vanguard of a zombie apocalypse – like the six million Shylocks of the heteronymous zombie memoir we've been tracking by fits and starts.

The decency and modesty (respectability) of translatability relies on the exclusion of such threats – the erection and codification of walls, fences, moats, demilitarized zones around the perimeter, as in the bad old days (pre-1797) of the Venetian Jews being confined within the walls of the Campo di Ghetto Nuovo.

Because Napoleon removed the gated walls around the Ghetto and made the Jews full citizens of Venice, the Portia Brigade in my story has no recourse against the six million Shylocks when they arrive. The Jewish zombies have flooded the city before the Portias have a chance to mobilize against them. No one knows where they come from, but they emerge out of the dozens of secret passageways dug and brick-lined by the confined Jews in centuries past. And when the Portia Brigade with their tommy guns[28] take up defensive positions around the Ghetto, and mow down the hordes of Shylocks in the tens of thousands, piling up the bodies in the square, the Shylocks reverse direction, flee back into the secret passageways, which make it possible for them to outflank the Portias just outside the armed perimeter, and to slaughter their attackers and eat their brains (finally getting their respective pounds of flesh).

Six Million Shylocks: A Zombie Memoir, Part 5.6
By Jacques Derrida
Pseudotranslated by Douglas Robinson

The Shylocks continued to pour out of the houses around the square. The sheer quantity of zombiehood in the square at any given time beggared the imagination – and they were all on their way out of the Ghetto. And more kept coming, so that the square was constantly full to bursting.

The only murderous flesh-eating incidents we saw now, however, were on the young woman's phone. Tourists were all now duly terrified. Those who had been wandering about the Campo di Ghetto Nuovo were presumably hiding on high floors of the buildings around the square – or dead.

Or undead.

* * *

We stood watching for several hours. Some gathered in small groups, gabbing obsessively, with a muted intensity. Panic laced the speech of a few; those around the panickers tried to calm them down.

---

[28] The fact that the head Portia in the zombie memoir calls the tommy guns "Chicago typewriters" – an old nickname for the tommy gun, from the Prohibition Era – is a hint that this is a *literary* zombie apocalypse. Indeed a pseudotranslational zombie apocalypse: no real-world island cities were injured in the pseudotranslating of the story. And the Shylocks are mindless undead bodies only in the mindfulness of story-translating. [Tr]

How is a footnote in the article *about* the zombie memoir to be understood as written by the pseudo-"Tr[anslator]" *of* the memoir? Wasn't it written by the "Au[thor]" of the article? [Au]

A deep unease weighed heavily on all of us. We all believed, I think, that we were in no immediate danger from the zombies. They were targeting Christians and sparing Jews. No, we worried about the repercussions from the Christians that survived. History had etched that fear into our hearts.

We had come out at dusk; now it was a starless night.

We were already talking about going inside when we began to hear gunfire. The Christian Venetians fighting back, we said. At first the shots were off in the distance. Soon, however, the "Zombie Patrol," as the news aggregators on the various cell phones were calling it – we were already referring to it as the Portia Brigade – began to set up stations around the perimeter of the Campo di Ghetto Nuovo and to gun down the Shylocks nearest them. We quickly realized that stray bullets would soon be flying our way. We went inside.

And indeed, within minutes we began to hear the staccato crackle of machine-gun fire. Rat-a-tat-tat all around the square. The videos featured on the Internet news aggregators showed them gunning down the Shylocks in the thousands.

I felt odd – out of joint, like Hamlet. The dissonance between the beautiful old historic synagogue in which we took shelter and what was transpiring outside seemed to take me out of my body. I walked to one wall, pressed my upper body against it, ran both hands over the ancient wood surface. *This is real*, I said to myself, over and over. *This is real*.

Not a particularly poststructuralist thought.

Since the Campo di Ghetto Nuovo was Ground Zero, or Patient Zero, or however one describes the hypocenter of a zombie apocalypse, the Portias would understandably take up positions around the periphery here, trying to stanch the flood at its source.

When a few bullets did crash through the synagogue's windows, we moved quickly out of the sanctuary and into the offices. There someone turned on a television, and we watched the coverage on CNN International. Its anchors were now calling the zombie apocalypse "Six Million Shylocks" – the first explicit historical link back from the invasion of Jewish zombies to the Holocaust, the Sho'ah.

* * *

And then we heard noises from the sanctuary. Cautiously, those nearest the door to the sanctuary opened it a crack and reported back on what they saw.

The Shylocks were now pouring back into the synagogue – and fleeing down the secret passageway.

I asked Rabbi Abravanel whether this was the only secret passageway out of the square, and he snorted a little.

"Of course not," he said. "There are dozens."

He expressed his guess that the Shylocks would now circle back around and outflank the Portias.

"One thing I've been wondering," I said, "is where the secret passageways run. Surely the soil under the city is not dry enough to sustain watertight tunnels?"

Rabbi Abravanel nodded. "Perhaps you've heard," he said, "of the Venice sewer system?"

"I don't believe I have," I said.

"In the sixteenth century, *gatoli* were run underground to handle sewage and rainwater."

"*Gatoli*?"

"Brick tunnels. Emptying into the canals and ultimately the lagoon."

"I see. But surely you don't mean that human beings *share* those sewage tunnels?"

"No, no, of course not. But beginning around Shakespeare's time, we began digging new tunnels and bricking them in for our people to use as secret escape routes."

"Hm. And do those tunnels span the canals as well, under water?"

"No," he said, with a slight shrug. "The secret passageways remain within the Ghetto Nuovo. Fleeing from persecutors was always a bit of a shell game."

I pictured the brick tunnels in my mind. Dark. Damp. Moldy. Trickles of greenish water running down the mortar joints. I pictured the Shylocks pelting through the tunnels, the *gatoli*. I imagined them panting gruffly, coughing, snorting, moaning, bent over at the waist, each Shylock's head pressed up against the backside of the Shylock in front of him. The awkward shuffle, the disjointed shamble. The blank determination on their undead faces.

I shook off the images.

"Then," I said, bringing myself back to the matter at hand, "do I take it you're assuming that the Shylocks will be able to outflank the Portias without leaving the Ghetto? Sneaking up behind them from the Ghetto side of each canal?"

"It's a big assumption, I agree," the rabbi said.[29]

---

[29] This assumption is especially "big" given the fact that there is no perimeter street around the ghetto. There are two bridges leaving the ghetto, the Ponte de Ghetto Novo (Bridge of the New Ghetto) to

"And," I added, "I'm guessing you have no idea where they came from in the first place? That first one emerged from the secret passageway into the synagogue – but it's a mystery where he *entered* that passageway?"

"I'm afraid so," he said.

* * *

CNN International (out of the Rome office) was showing an interview with the commanding officer of the Portia Brigade – apparently a dark-haired young man, but our Shakespearean nickname for the brigade made us suspect he was a woman in disguise.

"I'm speaking with Vitto Arvanitachi," the reporter was saying in English, "commanding officer of the Zombie Patrol, which has had remarkable success turning back the tide of zombies attacking Venice. CO Arvanitachi, for the record, is your name Vittorio or Vittoria?"

"Yes," V.A. said curtly.

"I see," the reporter said, swallowing hard. "We see before us, littering the square, the tens of thousands of zombies that you have laid low here in the Campo di Ghetto Nuovo, and now the tide has seemed to turn. Last we saw, the zombies were running for their – er, lives . . . "

"Yes," V.A. said, strutting a bit. "They seem to have had enough. Our Chicago typewriters took the stuffing right out of those undead monsters."

"Excuse me, Chicago typewriters?"

"Sorry, our trench brooms."

"Trench brooms?"

"What word are you looking for? Our tommy guns. Thompson SMGs."

"SMGs?"

"Submachine guns."

"Right, right. Yes, your SMGs cleared the square quite effectively. But what next?"

"Well, Alice," V. A. began, but just then a huge meat cleaver flashed on screen and split Vitto's skull like an overripe cantaloupe. A yellow-capped Shylock scooped out generous handfuls of brain and smashed them into his mouth. All along the line cleavers were splitting skulls and zombie

---

the right and the Ponte de Ghetto Vecchio (Bridge of the Old Ghetto) straight ahead and around to the left – and those bridges are the only access to the canals. Everywhere else, all the way around the island, the canal-side exterior walls of the buildings plunge right down into the water. If the underground passageways had let out next to the two bridges – out a window at the west end of the Italian synagogue, say – a single Portia could have stood on each bridge near the exits and picked the Shylocks off one by one as they emerged from the tunnels.

There is simply no realistic way the events in the climax to this story could have unfolded. The only reasonable conclusion is that "Derrida" made it all up – that it's sheer fantasy. [Tr]

fingers were fishing out brains and stuffing them greedily between bloody lips. Within seconds a good fifty or sixty Portias breathed no more.

We were craning to see whether the Shylocks had incapacitated the full Portia Brigade when, all of a sudden, the CNN reporter dropped her mic and bolted. Before she had taken three steps we heard a gruesome crunch and the camera dropped to the cobblestones and went dark.

A card with a graphic of a dog yanking a camera power cord out of the wall and the text TECHNICAL DIFFICULTIES PLEASE STAND BY popped up on the screen. Then the anchors in the Rome studio returned to tsk their tongues over the incident.

"I'm scratching my head here," the vaguely Asian-looking woman said, "trying to figure out why Alice interrupted her on-screen report with no warning."

"Well, yes, indeed," the vaguely North-African-looking man said. "And that is *no* way to handle an expensive video camera!"

* * *

"Looks like you were right, Rabbi," I said, trying hard to swallow the knot in my throat. "The Shylocks did manage to outflank the Portias."

"Indeed," the rabbi nodded. There seemed to be a similar knot in his throat too. How do you talk about a sight like that? A night like this?

"Horrific," he said, his voice throttled with emotion. "Just horrific footage."

I murmured my agreement.

"I have to admit, though," he mused, that chaos inside him dancing at the corners of his eyes, "that, unpleasant as it is, anyone who has suffered through the merciless dismantling of Shylock in Shakespeare's play. . ."

He paused.

"Yes?" I said.

"Well," he said, as if trying to convince himself to say it. "Any Jew in the audience at *The Merchant of Venice* will inevitably find some – some small morsel of satisfaction in that decimation of the Portia Brigade."

"Ouch," I said, grimacing. "Can we not use the word 'morsel,'[30] please?"

"Yes, sorry, you're so right, Professor." But the wild smile was still in his eyes. "I wasn't thinking."

But, I thought, he was right.

* * *

---

[30] Derrida's French word that I have translated "morsel" is *bouchée* (*trouver une petite bouchée de satisfaction*), or "bite, morsel, mouthful." [Tr]

"You know what occurs to me," I said.

"What's that?"

"The Shylocks wanted their pound of flesh. They came back for it."

He nodded. "Better late than never," he said.

* * *

The Night of the Six Million Shylocks continued on many fronts. There were more armed engagements. There were vicious attacks on defenseless and soon brainless goyim. Whole posses of Shylocks, often a good eighty to a hundred strong, would search through a building, finding and eating the hiding Gentiles.

Most alarming, perhaps, was the aquatic adventure. Several thousand Shylocks began diving into the lagoon and undermining the foundations of Venice's already infamously sinking buildings. We could not see what precisely they were doing – no one managed to send an underwater film crew down with a diving spotlight to record the destruction – but on the surface of the water it looked like the feeding frenzy of a million piranhas. The water seemed to boil. Within ten or fifteen minutes a whole large building would begin to tilt and sink. Were they digging with their undead hands? Were they biting the dirt with their undead teeth? We couldn't tell. But the buildings came down.

Sometimes victims would jump from the windows as the building they were hiding in collapsed into the lagoon. Then it was a simple matter for the Shylocks to harvest the swimmer, typically right there in the water, like a field amputation.

The Venice skyline began to change rather drastically.

5.7 An Alternate Ending to "Six Million Shylocks"

As "I" (??) originally wrote the story, the Portias circle the wagons in an attempt to keep the Shylocks not *in* the Jewish Campo di Ghetto Nuovo but *out* of a Christian enclave. Instead of killing all the zombies inside the perimeter, they face outward and gun down all the zombies trying to force their way in.

Jacques Derrida, however – our narrator and supposed author of the "memoir" of the night of the six million Shylocks – wants to let the zombies in.

Not only that: he recognizes that the zombies are always already in.

The very act of excluding the Shylock zombies gives them the power to undermine – negatively condition – not just the methods of relevant translatability but its philosophy, its theory, its ethos.

The general of the Anti-Zombie Force, Portia – the Supreme Portia in charge of the Portia Brigade, the most brilliant shape-shifter (man, woman, spotted hyena, Komodo dragon, Tasmanian devil) of all the highly trained shape-shifting Portias – mobilizes her letter-of-the-law Christian troops around the perimeter, armed to the teeth, with orders to blast any Shylock that approaches the wall. This campaign is wildly successful. Soon tens of thousands of Shylocks lie maimed and mutilated in the street, staining the cobblestones with their dark blood. The brigade has laid in vast stockpiles of ammunition, and as they keep repelling the zombie hordes, they don't run out of ammo. They keep reloading and firing and the Shylocks keep dying the second death.

But to the force's horror, every murderous fusillade revivifies zombies inside the wall. No one can tell where they're coming from. They seem to be popping out of nowhere.

It's harder to kill the zombies inside the compound. The Portias never seem to have a clean shot. The Supreme Portia tasks a whole battalion, 500 troops, with hand-to-hand combat, and issues each Portia a gleaming new meat cleaver from the mountain of cleavers beside her; the troops set about cleaving skulls. Many Shylocks manage to fall on their attackers, even with brainpans gaping open, and feast with their dying strength on their attackers' faces.

The Shylocks in their black gaberdines and yellow caps tend to mill five or six rows deep around workspaces where human translators are working, distracting the humans, moaning in their ears, swaying back and forth, jostling the translators' fingers off the home position on their keyboards.

Most of the translators are frantic with these distractions. They try to type faster, to finish their jobs by the deadline, keep them relevant.

But one translator seems to be in his element.

That would be Jacques Derrida, who has tunneled into the compound with a *pelle* "shovel," *par l'enlève et le relève de la terre à la pelle* "by shoveling the dirt up and out." Sometimes it seems as if his typing – on a manual typewriter! – revivifies the Shylocks. They are slithering out from between the keys. He moans along with them. He moans out Shylock's lines from a French translation by Jean-Michel Déprats (2011) that was published seven years after his death –

Œǣǣǣǣ̃[31] Juiiiiif n'a-t-il paaaaaaas des jøøøøøøøøøø?[32]

Un Juiiiiif n'a-t-il pas des mẽẽẽẽẽẽẽẽẽs,[33] des orgaaaaaanes, des dimãããããsjõõõõõõõns,[34] de sãããããns,[35] de l'affectijõõõõõõõn,[36] de la passijõõõõõõõn?[37]

Si vouuuuuus nouuuuuus piqueeeeez, ne saignons-nous paaaaaas?

---

[31] *Un.* [Tr] [32] *Yeux.* [Tr] [33] *Mains.* [Tr] [34] *Dimensions.* [Tr] [35] *Sens.* [Tr]
[36] *Affection.* [Tr] [37] *Passion.* [Tr]

– and the Shylock zombies emit a moaning kind of cheer.

His mẽẽẽẽẽẽẽẽẽs (*mains* = hands) try to integrate the zombies' moaaaaans into his translation, seeking ways of stylizing the moans so that they distract from the transmission of semantic sense, teach him ways of twisting that sense, turning it/them into blunt puns, hapless aporias, hand dystonias, stammers, grunts, humorously spastic leaps.

He too is often distracted. All around him cleavers flash and hot dark blood gushes. His sly glee will sometimes slip back into confusion, bafflement, a kind of "relevant" mental fog.

Could he be a zombie too?

Six Million Shylocks: A Zombie Memoir, Part 5.7
By Jacques Derrida
Pseudotranslated by Douglas Robinson

Rabbi Abranavel and I stayed up all night. A few others stuck it out as well, younger people, mainly. It felt a little like the end of a wild party, where you're too exhausted, physically and morally, to sort out the bad things that had happened from the possible consequences of those things.

I was so punchy by the time the sun started coming up that I hardly even noticed when it was that my mind drifted back to the Q&A session after my talk – to the idea that writing something up, writing up the taking up of a challenge, reacting or responding in writing to real-world events might have the real-world effect of restoring or rebuilding, and that that writing-something-up might work the same way in translation.

Could I, by translating this Italian and Sephardic world in Venice and Shakespeare's English world in *The Merchant of Venice* into French, and then into my translator's English,[38] have visited this Shylock zombie apocalypse upon a literary Venice?

The question I had to keep asking myself was this: If the *relève* of my visit to Venice visited that zombie apocalypse on Venice, what exactly did my writing up of the six million Shylocks tearing down Venice rebuild or restore? Should Shylock's collective revenge for the Sho'ah count as a restoration?

---

[38] The obvious question to ask here is what exactly Derrida means by "my translator's English." If he means "the English of my translator," referring to me and my English, how could *he* have "visited this Shylock zombie apocalypse on a literary Venice" by means of *my* translation? And if he means *his own* "translator's English," is he implying that he translated this story into English and only visited the Shylock zombie apocalypse on the literary Venice *of* and *in* this story? [Tr]

Conclusion

One way of summing up this essay might be to say that its zombies are mainly an imagistic intensification of "body," or "corporeality," or "physicality." To the extent that Christian mind–body dualism tends to equate mind or spirit or sense with translatability and "the body" or "the letter" or "the word" with untranslatability, zombie translations might be reduced to various translational literalisms, and the book as a whole might be debunked as just a weird way of echoing Venuti (2003/2013: 59) insisting that "Qu'est-ce qu'une traduction 'relevante'?" "addresses one of the most practical themes in the history of translation theory, notably the antithesis between 'word-for-word' and 'sense-for-sense' translation which occupied such writers as Cicero and Jerome."

But my zombie Shylocks are not only that. Not only do they resist reduction to stable binaries; they *eat* stable binaries from the inside out, like rhizomatic rats. The secret underground passageways by which they elude semantic capture are their rhizomatic burrows.

They are figures of embodied traumatic memories in uncanny repetition-compulsions. They keep coming back. They are as difficult to banish as an infestation of ants.

Above all, they are figures of what Michael Levine (2022) calls the (counter-)transferential working of Hegelian dialectics, whereby "something inside them seems to work against them, something that secretly, silently, and insistently undermines and reworks them from the inside out" (13).

If mind is thesis, body is antithesis, and objectified spirit is synthesis, zombies are not just "body" but the recursion of disgustingly embodied revenants in the interstices of that dialectical movement, interrupting and disrupting not just the sweep toward spirit but the very objectification of spirit.

If sense-for-sense translation is thesis, word-for-word translation is antithesis, and Relevant Translatability (the "best possible"!) is synthesis, philosophical zombies eat the brain of the invisible prompter that makes that synthesis *seem* possible. Zombies are the mindless body of the untranslatable that resists and confounds the triumph of Christian/Hegelian Idealism – including, downstream, that compromised idealism that gives us "relevant translation."

As Jacques Derrida himself might have put it, had he pushed a little harder on the body of his singular idiomatic words and the disturbing images of the Hegelian haunt, revenant zombie translation is itself *l'épreuve de l'intraduisible* "the trial of the untranslatable."

References

Austin, J. L. 1962/1975. *How To Do Things with Words*. Edited by J. O. Urmson and Marina Sbisà. Cambridge, MA: Harvard University Press.

Bakhtin, Mikhail. 1929/1984. *Problems of Dostoevsky's Poetics*. Translated and edited by Caryl Emerson. Minneapolis: University of Minnesota Press.

Bass, Alan, trans. 1987. Jacques Derrida, "To Speculate – on 'Freud'." In Jacques Derrida, *The Post Card*, 257–410. Chicago: University of Chicago Press.

Batchelor, Kathryn. 2023. "Re-reading Jacques Derrida's 'Qu'est-ce qu'une traduction "relevante"?' (What is a 'Relevant' Translation?)." *The Translator* 29.1: 1–16. doi.org/10.1080/13556509.2021.2004686.

Benjamin, Walter. 1923/1972. "Die Aufgabe des Übersetzers." In Tillman Rexroth, ed., *Kleine Prosa, Baudelaire-Übertragungen*, 9–21. Vol. 4, Part 1 of Walter Benjamin, *Gesammelte Schriften*. Frankfurt am Main: Suhrkamp.

Blackburn, John. 1958/1961. *A Scent of New-Mown Hay*. London: Penguin.

Block, Ned. 1978. "Troubles with Functionalism." *Minnesota Studies in the Philosophy of Science* 9: 261–325.

Block, Ned. 1995. "On a Confusion about a Function of Consciousness." *Behavioral and Brain Sciences* 18: 227–47.

Bolduc, Michelle. 2023. "The Relevance of Derrida's Translation: Mercy and Ethos." *The Translator* 29.4: 449–63. doi.org/10.1080/13556509.2023.2249164.

Borowicz, Jan. 2015. "Holocaust Zombies: Mourning and Memory." In Tanja Schult and Diana I. Popescu, eds., *Revisiting Holocaust Representation in the Post-Witness Era*, 132–48. London: Palgrave Macmillan.

Brandom, Robert B. 2002, *Tales of the Mighty Dead: Historical Essays in the Metaphysics of Intentionality*, Cambridge, MA: Harvard University Press.

Brandom, Robert B. 2014. "Some Hegelian Ideas of Note for Contemporary Analytic Philosophy." *Hegel Bulletin* 35.1: 1–15.

Brandom, Robert. 2019. *A Spirit of Trust: A Reading of Hegel's Phenomenology*. Cambridge, MA: Harvard University Press.

Carey, M. R. 2014. *The Girl with All the Gifts*. London: Orbit Books.

Chalmers, David. 1996. *The Conscious Mind: In Search of a Fundamental Theory*. Oxford: Oxford University Press.

Dan, Joseph. 1986. "Midrash and the Dawn of Kabbalah." In Geoffrey H. Hartman and Sanford Budick, eds., *Midrash and Literature*, 127-39. New Haven: Yale University Press.

Davis, Kathleen. 2001. *Deconstruction and Translation*. Manchester: St Jerome.

Déprats, Jean-Michel, trans. 2011. William Shakespeare, *Le Marchand de Venise*. Folio théâtre 116. Edited by Gisèle Venet. Paris: Gallimard.

Derrida, Jacques. 1977/1988. "Limited Inc a b c." In Jacques Derrida, *Limited Inc.*, 29–110. Edited by Gerald Graff. Evanston: Northwestern University Press.

Derrida, Jacques. 1985. "Des Tours de Babel" (in French). In Joseph F. Graham, ed., *Difference in Translation*, 209–48. Ithaca, NY: Cornell University Press.

Derrida, Jacques. 1999. "Qu'est-ce qu'une traduction 'relevante'?" *Quinzièmes Assises de la Traduction Littéraire (Arles 1998)*, 21–48. Arles: Actes Sud.

Derrida, Jacques. 2019. *Séminaire (1997–1998)*. Vol. 1 of *Le parjure et le pardon*. Paris: Seuil.

Derrida, Jacques. 2020. *Séminaire (1998–1999)*. Vol. 2 of *Le parjure et le pardon*. Paris: Seuil.

Ertel, Emmanuel. 2011. "Derrida on Translation and His (Mis)reception in America." *Trahir* (September): 1–18.

Freud, Sigmund. 1997. "The Theme of the Three Caskets." In Sigmund Freud, *Writings on Art and Literature*, 109–21. Stanford: Stanford University Press.

Goethe, Johann Wolfgang von. 1826/1907. *Maximen und Reflexionen: Nach den Handschriften des Goethe- und Schiller-Archivs*. Edited by Max Hechter. Weimar: Verlag der Goethe-Gesellschaft. https://ia800209.us.archive.org/18/items/goethemaximenun00goetgoog/goethemaximenun00goetgoog.pdf. Accessed September 5, 2020.

Golffing, Francis, trans. 1956. Friedrich Nietzsche, "The Genealogy of Morals: An Attack." In *The Birth of Tragedy and The Genealogy of Morals*, 147–299. New York: Anchor/Doubleday.

Gomel, Elana. 2024. "Corpses of Memory: Holocaust Zombies." https://medium.com/@maya1233/corpses-of-memory-holocaust-zombies-26ddb83cdb05 (Part 1: "Memory and History"), https://medium.com/@maya1233/corpses-of-memory-holocaust-zombies-d4cb8c2d1aef (Part 2: "Fungal Utopias"), https://medium.com/@maya1233/corpses-of-memory-holocaust-zombies-58047906cd24; (Part 3: "Return of the Dead Jews"). Accessed November 21, 2024.

Graham, Joseph F., trans. 1985. "Des Tours de Babel" (in English). In Joseph F. Graham, ed., *Difference in Translation*, 165–205. Ithaca, NY: Cornell University Press.

Han, Byung-Chul. 2024. *The Crisis of Narration*. Hoboken, NJ: Polity Press.

Hermans, Theo. 2014. *The Conference of the Tongues*. London: Routledge.

Jannès-Kalinowski, Isabelle, trans. 2016. Igor Ostachowicz, *La nuit des Juifs-vivants*. Paris: Édicions L'Antilope.
Kripke, Saul. 1972/1980. *Naming and Necessity*. Cambridge, MA: Harvard University Press.
Langer, Lawrence. 1995. *Abiding the Holocaust: Collected Essays*. Oxford: Oxford University Press.
Levine, Michael G. 2022. "Translation, Transference, *Trouvaille*: Derrida's 'What is a 'Relevant' Translation?'" *Diacritics* 50.3: 4–28.
Lindqvist, John Ajvide. 2023. "She." In Margret Helgadottir, ed., *Nordic Visions: The Best of Nordic Speculative Fiction*, 15–47. London: Solaris.
Littau, Karin. 2016. "Translation and the Materialities of Communication." *Translation Studies* 9.1: 82–96.
Luckhurst, Roger. 2016. *Zombies: A Cultural History*. London: Reaktion Books.
McDowell, John. H. 2006. "The Apperceptive I and the Empirical Self: Towards a Heterodox Reading of 'Lordship and Bondage' in Hegel's *Phenomenology*." In Katerina Deligiorgi, ed., *Hegel: New Directions*, 33–48. Chesham: Acumen.
McDowell, John. H. 2018. "What is the *Phenomenology* About?" In Federico Sanguinetti and Andre J. Abath, eds., *McDowell and Hegel: Perceptual Experience, Thought and Action*, 29–42. Cham: Springer.
Milesi, Laurent, trans. 2012. Hélène Cixous, "Shakespeare Ghosting Derrida." *Oxford Literary Review* 34.1: 1–24. doi.org/10.3366/olr.2012.0027.
Nicholson-Smith, Donald, trans. 1973. Jean Laplanche and Jean-Bertrand Pontalis, eds., *The Language of Psychoanalysis*. New York: Norton.
Ostachowicz, Igor. 2012. *Noc żywych Żydów*. Warsaw: Wydawnictwo W. A. B.
Philippi, Donald. 1989. "Translation between Typologically Diverse Languages." *Meta: journal des traducteurs/Meta: Translators' Journal* 34.4: 680–85.
Pinkard, Terry. 1994. *Hegel's Phenomenology: The Sociality of Reason*. Cambridge, UK: Cambridge University Press.
Pinkard, Terry. 2000. *Hegel: A Biography*. Cambridge, UK: Cambridge University Press.
Pinkard, Terry. 2012. *Hegel's Naturalism: Mind, Nature, and the Final Ends of Life*. New York: Oxford University Press.
Pippin, Robert B. 1989. *Hegel's Idealism: The Satisfactions of Self-Consciousness*. Cambridge, UK: Cambridge University Press.
Pippin, Robert R. 2010. *Hegel on Self-Consciousness: Desire and Death in the Phenomenology of Spirit*. Princeton: Princeton University Press.

Pippin, Robert B. 2019. *Hegel's Realm of Shadows: Logic as Metaphysics in the Science of Logic*. Chicago: University of Chicago Press.

Pym, Anthony. 2010. *Exploring Translation Theories*. London: Routledge.

Reynolds, Matthew. 2019. "Prismatic Agon, Prismatic Harmony: Translation, Literature, Language." In Matthew Reynolds, ed., *Prismatic Translation*, 21–47. Cambridge, UK: Modern Humanities Research Association.

Robinson, Douglas. 1996. *Translation and Taboo*. DeKalb: Northern Illinois University Press.

Robinson, Douglas, ed. 2014. *Western Translation Theory from Herodotus to Nietzsche*. London: Routledge.

Robinson, Douglas. 2017. *Exorcising Translation: Towards an Intercivilizational Turn*. London: Bloomsbury Academic.

Robinson, Douglas. 2022. "Heteronymous Narratoriality: The Translator (as Narrator) as Somebody Else." *Cultus* 15: 56–75.

Robinson, Douglas. 2023. *Translation as a Form: A Centennial Commentary on Walter Benjamin's "Task of the Translator."* London: Routledge.

Robinson, Douglas. 2024. "The Communality of Interepistemic Translation: Charles Sanders Peirce and Thomas Kuhn on the Interepistemicity of Scientific Communities." *Translation Matters* 6.2 (Autumn): 154–77.

Stoljar, David. 2018. "The Epistemic Approach to the Mind–Body Problem." www.youtube.com/watch?v=qqJFEWEi148&t=4319s. Accessed November 27, 2024.

Stratton, Jon. 2017. "Trouble with Zombies: *Muselmänner*, Bare Life, and Displaced People." In Sarah Juliet Lauro, ed., *Zombie Theory: A Reader*, 246–71. Minneapolis: University of Minnesota Press.

Toury, Gideon. 2012. *Descriptive Translation Studies – and Beyond*. Amsterdam: John Benjamins.

Venuti, Lawrence. 2001a. "Introduction." *Critical Inquiry* 27.2: 169–73. doi .org/10.1086/449004.

Venuti, Lawrence, trans. 2001b. Jacques Derrida, "What is a 'Relevant' Translation?" *Critical Inquiry* 27.2: 174-200.

Venuti, Lawrence. 2003/2013. "Translating Derrida on Translation: Relevance and Disciplinary Resistance." In Lawrence Venuti, ed., *Translation Changes Everything. Theory and Practice*, 57–79. London: Routledge.

Venuti, Lawrence, trans. 2004. Jacques Derrida, "What is a 'Relevant' Translation?" In Lawrence Venuti, ed., *The Translation Studies Reader*, 2nd ed., 365–88. New York: Routledge.

Venuti, Lawrence, trans. 2012. Jacques Derrida, "What is a 'Relevant' Translation?" In Lawrence Venuti, ed., *The Translation Studies Reader*, 3rd ed., 365–88. New York: Routledge.

Vermeer, Hans. 2005. "Einige Antworten auf Derridas Frage, was eine relevante Übersetzung sei." *Lebende Sprachen* 50.: 116–19.

Vidal Claramonte, Maria Carmen África, and Tong King Lee. 2025. *Hypertranslation*. Cambridge, UK: Cambridge University Press.

Villaverde, Francisco Javier, trans. 2014. Igor Ostachowicz, *La noche de los judíos vivientes*. Barcelona: Nube de Tinta.

Weber, Samuel, and Jeffrey Mehlman, trans. 1977/1988. Jacques Derrida, "Limited Inc a b c." In Gerald Graff, ed., *Limited Inc.* Evanston: Northwestern University Press.

Wills, David, trans. 2022. Jacques Derrida, *Perjury and Pardon*, vol. 1. Edited by Ginette Michaud and Nicholas Cotton. Chicago: University of Chicago Press.

Wills, David, trans. 2023. Jacques Derrida, *Perjury and Pardon*, vol. 2. Edited by Ginette Michaud and Nicholas Cotton. Chicago: University of Chicago Press.

Thanks:
Zombie vector (Section divider) by Seamartini (royalty-free at vectorstock.com/ 52142326)

Cambridge Elements

Translation and Interpreting

The series is edited by Kirsten Malmkjær with Sabine Braun as associate editor for Elements focusing on Interpreting.

Kirsten Malmkjær
University of Leicester

Kirsten Malmkjær is Professor Emeritus of Translation Studies at the University of Leicester. She has taught Translation Studies at the universities of Birmingham, Cambridge, Middlesex and Leicester and has written extensively on aspects of both the theory and practice of the discipline. *Translation and Creativity* (London: Routledge) was published in 2020 and *The Cambridge Handbook of Translation*, which she edited, was published in 2022. She is preparing a volume entitled *Introducing Translation* for the Cambridge Introductions to Language and Linguistics series.

Editorial Board

Adriana Serban, *Université Paul Valéry*
Barbara Ahrens, *Technische Hochschule Köln*
Liu Min-Hua, *Hong Kong Baptist University*
Christine Ji, *The University of Sydney*
Jieun Lee, *Ewha Womans University*
Lorraine Leeson, *The University of Dublin*
Sara Laviosa, *Università Delgi Stuidi di Bari Aldo Moro*
Fabio Alves, *FALE-UFMG*
Moira Inghilleri, *University of Massachusetts Amherst*
Akiko Sakamoto, *University of Portsmouth*
Haidee Kotze, *Utrecht University*

About the Series

Elements in Translation and Interpreting present cutting edge studies on the theory, practice and pedagogy of translation and interpreting. The series also features work on machine learning and AI, and human-machine interaction, exploring how they relate to multilingual societies with varying communication and accessibility needs, as well as text-focused research.

Cambridge Elements

Translation and Interpreting

Elements in the Series

The Graeco-Arabic Translation Movement
El-Hussein A Y Aly

Interpreting as Translanguaging: Theory, Research, and Practice
Lili Han, Zhisheng (Edward) Wen, Alan James Runcieman

Creative Classical Translation
Paschalis Nikolaou

Translation as Creative–Critical Practice
Delphine Grass

Translation in Analytic Philosophy
Francesca Ervas

Towards Game Translation User Research
Mikołaj Deckert, Krzysztof W. Hejduk, and Miguel Á. Bernal-Merino

Hypertranslation
Mª Carmen África Vidal Claramonte and Tong King Lee

An Extraordinary Chinese Translation of Holocaust Testimony
Meiyuan Zhao

Researching and Modelling the Translation Process
Muhammad M. M. Abdel Latif

Risk Management in Translation
Anthony Pym

Literary Exophonic Translation
Lúcia Collischonn

A Zombie Theory of Translation: Or, What is a "Revenant" Translation?
Douglas Robinson

A full series listing is available at: www.cambridge.org/EITI

Printed by Integrated Books International,
United States of America